G-3722

# THE ART OF SUCCESSFUL TEACHING:

## A BLEND OF CONTENT & CONTEXT

———————•———————

## TIM LAUTZENHEISER

GIA PUBLICATIONS, INC.

# Dedication

This book is dedicated to every music director who has "dreamed the dream," and taken a few steps toward that wonderful vision with a child following closely behind.

Most of all, you should be thanked. It is a privilege for me to have you read this book. Thank you!

Portions of this book have appeared in slightly different form in the following publications: Music Educators Journal, Bandworld, The Instrumentalist, Today's Music Educator, BDGuide, and Let's Cheer. Reprinted with permission.

International Copyright Secured.
Library of Congress Catalog Card Number: 91-77572
ISBN: 941050-29-7
Printed in U.S.A.

# Contents

# Acknowledgements

It seems everyone aspires to be an author, doesn't it? Everyone wants to "leave something" which will make a positive impact on future generations, or perhaps draw attention to the contribution of the ideas within a book. It seems a bit presumptuous to think there will be any real change in the momentum of the world based on a few pages of thoughts. For the most part, people have their minds made up about the important issues, and the unimportant ones don't deserve much attention. It's my hope the following pages will cause some healthy introspection. That's really all that's intended.

We all know there is a balance in life and whenever anyone says, "White!" it is certain someone will shout back, "No, black!" In other words, there will be some things in this book you love and some you do not. It is merely a composite of thoughts and opinions. If this book provokes some thought or even argument, then we all have gained. The purpose of this book is to strengthen and support our continued commitment to achieving excellence in every aspect of our personal and professional lives.

Open the book anywhere and begin to read. Starting at page one and reading to the end will have no more value than beginning in the middle and going in both directions. This is a reference book for you to enjoy. Enjoy!

*When all is said and done, much is said and little is done.* More than anything, I hope the book will help you gain some personal understandings. There are lots of words in the following pages, but the real value concerns the actions we take based on the words.

## Thank-you's

Every book has a page of author thank-you's. In this case, everyone who has been involved in my growth process needs a pat on the back, either for contributing to the learning endeavor or putting up with me along the way.

# Author's Note

# The Art of Successful Teaching: A Blend of Content & Context

The title of this book represents the bridge between the cognitive and affective domain.

Successful teaching: is it *content* or *context*?

This particular question has been the topic of many late-night discussions and endless arguments since the beginning of education itself. Perhaps there will never be a clear-cut answer since the answer is not an "either-or," but rather a blend of both components.

We tend to choose sides based on our own educational background and yet when we observe the master teachers in action, it is difficult to distinguish which is of greater importance. This, of course, simply perpetuates the argument.

Let us assume the answer to the question is, "Yes." As of yet, we cannot measure intuitive (contextual) understanding, but we find this signature in our own lives and in our own teaching experiences. Inspirational teaching is not a part of most curriculums for the aspiring teacher; however, we are all drawn to the teacher who captures our attention.

Personally, I think we have avoided this important aspect of education since it is not measurable. Some rather remarkable contributions are now being made by our contemporary researchers in breaking down the various elements of inspired teaching. These researchers are literally outlining the individual facets of quality teaching and then creating a blueprint which will reliably uplift the learning experience for the students. The missing pieces of the puzzle are now being identified.

Though it may be a bit in the future, it is apparent we are going to be able to quantify the magic which some teachers bring to class. Although there are some who are naturally gifted, we can all develop our own personalities and become highly communicative teaching talents. It is a matter of blending content and context.

# Foreword
# by F. Earl Dunn

Tim Lautzenheiser, a small-town boy from Bluffton, Indiana, who took his snare drum to the Ball State University School of Music and became one of its most outstanding students, is recognized today as one of the nation's most dynamic and successful speakers.

Tim is known by thousands of students throughout the world and has had a career encompassing ten years as an outstanding conductor of bands at Northern Michigan University, the University of Missouri, and New Mexico State University. Colleagues have always recognized his concert and marching bands as a "step ahead of their times," establishing trends and styles for the future.

His nationally acclaimed performance organizations soon brought recognition from the music industry which, in turn, led to his appointment as Executive Director of Bands of America. During this period of his career, he was literally inundated with requests to present his popular leadership workshops to various organizations, so it seemed logical to establish Attitude Concepts for Today, Inc.

Tim is a rare and unique individual—sophisticated and worldly possessing an unbelievable blend of realism and idealism. He is articulate and entertaining and believes teaching is an art; a profession which allows you to have a positive influence on the lives of many.

He has never lost his aptitude for caring, an obvious throwback to his youth in Bluffton; and he sincerely believes young people have not really changed, only the times have. Tim's inspirational presentations have led literally thousands to believe—"if you think you can, you can." His work with teachers has made it possible for many to realize that there are not really problem students, but only problems/challenges in finding methods to communicate with them and motivate them. Yes, Tim *believes* students will reach unbelievable levels of excellence if teachers open the doors for learning.

It is hoped this book, which is a collection of Tim's articles, will have a positive influence on you, and remind you, "if you think you can, you can."

Today, when Tim is not on the road, he resides back home in Bluffton, Indiana with Andrea and his motivated and uninhibited Boxer, "Furlie."

## ABOUT F. EARL DUNN

The Foreword has been written by one of the most (if not "the most") influential teachers in my life, Mr. F. Earl Dunn, formerly Director of Bands at Ball State University and the University of Alabama. When we speak about the importance of role models, my thoughts always turn to my college band director, Mr. Dunn.

To this day, I still call him for advice, share my thoughts about various problems and seek his wisdom concerning the future. All of these he shares unselfishly and continues to serve as a mentor of cherished value.

Mr. Dunn is responsible for many of the fine music educators in our profession. His own career is a tribute to his commitment and dedication, and he has not only brought enlightenment to those of us who were lucky enough to spend time with him in rehearsal and the classroom, but he served as president of the National Band Association as well as countless other offices in the music world. He is a champion for me...and always will be.

Being an animal lover, it is not an accident that the cherished member of our family who always expresses unconditional love was named in honor of my favorite teacher. Our Boxer dog, "F-Earl" (Furlie) reminds all of us how important it is to enjoy life and make the most of each day.

A very special thanks to Mr. Dunn for, once again, extending his talents on behalf of "a student," and I will always be "your student" of life.

# Introduction
# by Barry Green

Think of the last time you participated in a truly inspiring musical performance. Were you thrilled at the level of your playing? When learning a new piece of solo music, can you recall the excitement of being able to play it for the first time? After the performance, the feeling of pride and exhilaration can sometimes stay with you for hours, days, or forever. Such memorable moments are not restricted to the concert stage and can be experienced in practicing, lessons, the classroom or such non-musical settings as sports events, theater, or movies.

These intense experiences produce a chemical (adrenaline) "rush" in the nervous system. This "rush" is so desirable that we may want to re-experience it as often as possible. It motivates us to learn, accomplish, perfect, succeed, participate, and enjoy the feeling over and over. It is one of those things that makes life fun!

At the mere mention of Tim Lautzenheiser, those of us who have been fortunate enough to meet him will probably smile and just begin to feel good inside. Why? Because Tim has given us some of these thrills (or rushes)! There are few people in this world who have reached out and not only touched us with inspiration but have the capacity to inspire change in us as well. Those of us who have personally experienced Tim know what I am describing.

If you have not met Tim in person, you will likely experience his energy and wonderful ideas in the pages that lie ahead. As you are about to read some of his book, there are many ways you can digest these pages. Your reading can be out of sequence, a paragraph here and another there. Read as little or as much as you like. However, the real question is, How will you process this information? Let me offer a suggestion: it is interesting to be informed, it is nice to be entertained, it is helpful to get some good advice, it is convenient to have some well-placed reading material that you can enjoy at will. However, if you really want a "rush," I would like to invite you to allow this book to come to life. After reading some of Tim's The Art of Successful Teaching, you may feel a sense of truth or identification with what he has described. This feeling of recognition can stay where it is or it can evolve to another level of action. The real thrill lies in what you can now do, perhaps in a new way that you have never done before. There is a big difference between "talking the talk" and "walking the walk." With new directions in education, learning, and performance, we can experience true satisfaction. You are the only person in this world who can allow yourself to experience something new through the creative inspiration of Tim's writing. Explore and discover and take risks. Have a breakthrough with the potential to allow you to experience the thrill of learning, the joy of accomplishment, the pleasure of improvement, and a rush of excitement. This is an opportunity to experience some new levels of our own potential through the examples and inspirational ideas Tim gives us in this book. Thank you, Tim, for making it accessible to us. Enjoy!

## ABOUT BARRY GREEN

Barry Green, author of The Inner Game of Music, is more than just a cherished friend. He is a person who has become a "thinking partner." He sees beyond the obvious parameters of music education and doesn't spend much time dwelling on "why it can't work," but instead focuses his energies on ways "to make it work."

Like most of us, Barry shares our greed for excellence, but Barry is seeking new and exciting ways to develop it. He is exploring unchartered territories and discovering new and exciting ways to bring about higher levels of performance and musical understanding. Barry Green is one of a kind and certainly marches to the beat of his own drum. I so admire his sense of purpose, his tenacity, and his extraordinary achievements. He is reminding all of us how important it is to "open our minds" as the certain pathway to musical success.

Above all, Barry Green has been a confidant as well as an encouraging force in my own quest. While some have stood on the sidelines with arched eyebrows and skepticism, Barry has always been the one to add fuel to my fire. Our intuitive communication gives great strength when the mind and body are weary. There is no doubt in my mind there is a connection here which is more than mere serendipity.

Thank you, my friend, for agreeing to write the introduction to this book. It is yet another favor which is an outgrowth of a friendship beyond words.

*You cannot stay on the summit forever; you have to come down again. So why bother in the first place? Just this: What is above knows what is below, but what is below does not know what is above. One climbs, one sees, one descends, one sees no longer...but one has seen. There is a way of conducting oneself in the lower regions by the memory of what one saw higher up: When one can no longer see, one can at least still know. We live and love by what we have seen.*

—*Rene Daumal*

# If You Think...You Can!

If you think you're beaten you are.
 If you think you dare not, you don't
If you'd like to win but think you can't,
 It's almost for sure you won't.

If you think you're losing, you've lost.
 For out in the world we find—
Success begins with a person's will.
 It's all in the state of mind.

If you think your outclassed, you are.
 You've got to think high to rise.
You have to stay with it,
 In order to win the prize.

Life's battles don't always go
 To the one with the better plan.
For more often than not, you will win
 If only you think you can.

# Part One

# The Art of Teaching

# The Art of Teaching

We're lucky if we have two or three great teachers in our lives! That's the truth! Remember your great ones? If you will take a moment and reflect on those educators who made a lasting impression, you will probably discover it was *not* the subject material which brought you to the front of your seat, it was the teacher...that magical person who could take technically boring information and make it live, create interest, tickle your inquisitive mind, and bring forth a desire to want more data.

One of the more popular phrases often heard in the halls of music schools around the nation is, "If you can't play, then you can teach." That always bothered me...still does! Teaching is an art in its own right. A great teacher can amass information of any kind and have students excited and interested in a topic, not so much because of the topic, but because of the presentation of the material, or, if you will, the performance of the teaching.

Being an "expert" on any subject matter does *not* a teacher make. We all have the example of our college professors who were the "international expert" on the given subject matter and had written the definitive text concerning that very topic. Yet, in the classroom, they failed time and time again to teach...they simply lectured. There was no sense of performance or art in conveying this information; in fact, it often seemed a burden to their schedule and they would much rather have been researching or writing. Likewise, we have all experienced that enthusiastic graduate student who could take the most elementary information and have everyone buzzing about what a fantastic class they were having.

Perhaps the art of teaching can't be taught. We can observe the "great ones" and record their body language, pacing, outlines, etc., but we cannot capture the spontaneity and the sensitivity which is so crucial to their success. They are artists in the strictest sense of the word, and they are not often recognized for this talent, but are overshadowed by others who are in a more visible area of performance.

The true teacher is one that teaches out of a passion for sharing. Teaching is a profession of service to other people. The word *care* seems to suggest the appropriate main theme of the artistic teachers: THEY CARE!

This section of the text is written with this theme in mind—the importance of the need *to care.*

*"The trouble with music appreciation in general is that people are taught to have too much respect for music; they should be taught to love it instead."*

# What Makes Great Teachers?

If we are fortunate, we will have three or four great teachers in our lives. Teachers who were able to touch something down deep inside us which really determined our thinking about everything. Perhaps they confirmed a certain belief pattern, or influenced the way we handled problems, caused us to understand a behavioral habit, etc. These were special educators—super teachers—gifted in shaping and directing our lives.

No doubt, many of us chose to become teachers because of these influential individuals. We wanted to follow in their footsteps and have used them as models in developing our own style of teaching.

What made these educators different from the other teachers? They went to the same colleges, took the same courses, parked in the same lot with the other faculty. They suffered the same budget cuts, took their turn at lunch-line duty, and had personal crises. Yet, there was something distinctively different, a certain *charisma* which separated this teacher from the masses.

Wouldn't it be wonderful if we could identify these qualities and pass them on to all teachers who could, in turn, have an equal impact on their students? Or think about taking a college methods course on "Techniques of Meaningful Life Direction via Classroom Material" or "Creating Personal Fulfillment and Purpose through My Classroom Experience." We would all sign up for those courses! What do you suppose the curriculum would be? What texts would they use? Who would teach the class? Would we study the Bible? Socrates? Plato? Would we research or do role playing experiments? How would we gain this important information which would ensure effective teaching?

In our educational world we have two basic areas of emphasis: *cognitive* (skills, facts, measurable information) and *affective* (attitudes, feelings, conceptual thinking). To help us determine the characteristics of these great teachers, let us be specific in identifying what made them stand out in our assessment of the countless educators who were a part of our formal learning. If you will take just a moment and remember one or two of your finest teachers, then focus on the attributes which gave them this personally-bestowed honor in your life. The list of qualities will probably look something like this:

1. They were CARING.
2. They showed tremendous DEDICATION.
3. They always HAD TIME for me.
4. They had a good SENSE OF HUMOR.
5. They could COMMUNICATE well.
6. They ENJOYED their work.
7. They showed PERSONAL DISCIPLINE.
8. They were FAIR.
9. They demonstrated PERSISTENCE.
10. They RESPECTED me as a person.

(And the list goes on and on...)

If we take this list and divide these qualities into *skills* and *attitudes*, it will give us some basis for determining the inherent characteristics of this extraordinary teacher. (Of course, all of this can be argued; however, let's bypass these "either/or" details in favor of coming to some conclusion which can benefit all of us.).

CARING. There's no question about this one. It's an *attitude*. It takes a certain amount of skill to maintain this attitude, but *caring* is a choice of behavior.

DEDICATION. Although maintaining any sort of dedication is a real *skill*, the people who are dedicated don't learn this from a text. If they weren't dedicated, they wouldn't be reading the texts in the first place. Dedication is at *attitude* about how we are going to spend our given time and with what intensity level we are going to focus our energy.

HAVING TIME TO SHARE. Certainly we are talking about a *major attitude* here. We all have the same amount of hours in the day. Any educator can decide how to spend those given hours. We all admire those unique teachers who welcome our personal thoughts and show sincere interest in us beyond the classroom.

SENSE OF HUMOR. Humor is the shortest distance between two people. The most effective humor stems from the enjoyment of the day-to-day situations which occur right under our noses. In most cases, we can either get upset about what happened or find some humor in it and move on. Humor releases tension, anger causes it. Definitely, a sense of humor is an *attitude*.

COMMUNICATION. We read a lot about "communicative skills," and certainly there is a lot to be said for understanding how to communicate. Yet, with all the skills in the world, little is exchanged unless we are ready to accept the responsibility of expressing ourselves. We all make a conscious choice to share or not to share. Therefore, communication becomes a skill fueled by an *attitude*.

ENJOYMENT. We may "learn" the habit of enjoyment, but for most people, enjoyment is a direct reflection of their *attitude*. People choose to enjoy opera, football, stamp collecting, gardening or whatever. They have a positive attitude about what they are doing. Others may learn (*skill*) all the ins and outs of a particular activity and still never enjoy one moment of their involvement.

21

PERSONAL DISCIPLINE. We all admire and respect the person who is willing to go the extra mile. And we all have this opportunity each and every day. There is no book on how to be disciplined. It is a matter of enforcing our will power. It's making up our mind to seek excellence. It's an *attitude* about how we want to live our lives.

FAIR. Many times our assessment of a fair teacher is one who broke existing rules because the rules were unfair in a given circumstance. Perhaps this teacher extended a deadline on a paper, or gave extra credit for dedicated service, even violated a school policy to see you have a better opportunity. Most certainly, this is an *attitude* about the student's best interests.

PERSISTENCE. This wonderful key to success is the very *attitude* which separates those who "know" from those who "succeed." These great examples simply will not give up! When all others throw in the towel (and justifiably so), here comes Master Teacher with two or three more efforts which, ultimately, sets the standards for all others. This quality represents a very simple choice: I won't quit! What a tremendous *attitude*.

RESPECT. Teachers who respect their students also respect themselves. We cannot give to others what we don't have for ourselves. No academic degree or position can give you respect. Respect is something which comes from within. It is an *attitude* about oneself which transfers directly to those around us. So often, we think attending this or that workshop, clinic, or seminar will make us more effective teachers—when, in fact, we should be thinking: This new information will give me more to share with my students via my effective teaching.

As we have discovered, those quality mentors were the ones who displayed incredible attitudes. We all have experienced teachers who were knowledgeable (beyond compare) yet were totally ineffective in the classroom situation. We respected their bank of facts, but eagerly looked forward to the completion of the class so we could get on with life. Then there were those magical teachers who brought us to the edge of our seats, often in subject areas where we had no specific interest other than getting caught up in the enthusiasm reflected from this compelling force, the teacher!

All of us want to improve our teaching effectiveness. (If we don't, perhaps we're not real teachers in the first place!) There is no question we will continue to sharpen our skills, for this is the way we grow, learn, create, and become more qualified to do our best work. These skills offer us the ability to move forward in our purpose. However, these skills are virtually worthless in our educational system unless they are used in the correct fashion and with the proper attitude.

If we are destined to make a positive difference in the lives of our students, then we must develop those qualities which are the trademarks of the Master Teacher: positive, productive attitudes!

The exciting part of all of this lies in the fact that when we accept this reality, we not only become better teachers, we improve our own lives, which in turn allows us to be more effective in the classroom, and the cycle goes on and on. It's ironic, but the truth is: We are the only teacher we have ever had! Let's give ourselves a greater education via great attitudes!

Here's to teaching *excellence!*

*"Unless you know to what port you sail, no wind is a good wind. Remember too, that winds change with each day and sails are trimmed to meet existing winds."*

# Worth Our Weight in Goals!

"There is just never enough time! It seems I just finish taking roll when the bell rings. The frustration is driving me nuts!"

"Each year I promise myself not to get entangled in this trap of always being behind and never getting caught up, but it just seems to be a pattern I can't break. How do other teachers get everything done?"

"If someone would just tell me one thing I could count on to really help with this situation of too much to do and not enough time to do it in, it would be worth everything to me."

Have you ever heard these all-too-familiar statements? Perhaps they have even passed through your lips. They seem to be inherent in the profession, don't they? How does one stay on top of the situation and not fall prey to the anxiety caused by constant incompletion of work?

Goal-setting is nothing revolutionary in the educational world. In fact, we have all memorized the "benefit package" available to the individual who establishes goals. And, most certainly, we all have goals. Our students have goals. Our schools have goals. Everyone has goals. However, in looking a step further, it is evident that successful teachers maintain a serious disciplined pattern when it comes to short- and long-term goal setting. Their consistently high level of accomplishment serves as a positive testimony to the worth of this process. The exercise does pay off.

Studies in brain dominance, bio-feedback, autogenic programming, and other facets of human behavior confirm that the subconscious mind cannot distinguish between fact and fiction and sends the conscious mind whatever data it receives—thus the statement "Whether we think we can, or whether we think we can't, we're always right." We harvest exactly what we plant. The behavior is in direct correlation to the thoughts we plant in your minds each day.

Do we carefully plan our day? Specifically design our week of rehearsals? Outline the first and second priority goals of the month, the semester, the year? Or, are we flying by the seat of our pants? It is an uncomfortable set of questions, isn't it? How quickly we are reminded of that familiar quote: "Failing to plan means planning to fail."

We will spend hours selecting the "perfect" music for the upcoming concert, but will not extend that same detailed preparation in the planning of the rehearsal format. Not only is this self-defeating, but it becomes a vicious circle leading to personal stress, poor performances, strained rehearsals, and a constant battle for program survival. These negative results confirm our worst fears, and reinforce the subconscious mind. Further, the cycle is certain to repeat itself, even though everyone involved never wants it to happen again. (A classic case of self-fulfilling prophecy.)

How does one break the cycle? What steps can be taken to alter this seemingly endless, predictable outcome? The answer might well be within the logic of these questions:

Would you start driving across the country without a map?

Would you attempt to put together a jig-saw puzzle without the picture on the box?

Have you ever boarded a plane not knowing its destination?

How ridiculous and simplistic these questions appear! Only a fool would be lured into such nonsense.

Our mind leads us in the direction of its most dominant thought. Are we taking control of those thoughts and carefully "mapping out" our future, or are we simply a talented library of musical understanding hoping everything will fall in place?

It is imperative that we set the goals—draw our map, define the intent, lay out the plans, create the blueprint—which will determine the success of our efforts.

The mind works on goals like a homing pigeon. Without a destination, the homing pigeon is known to fly in circles until it collapses in a heat of exhaustion. It is time to focus our efforts, just as we would focus a camera before taking a photograph to insure a clean, crisp representation of the vision.

Setting goals—creating our vision in detail—is more than just "thinking through" what the day has in store on our way to school. It is a highly skilled procedure with strict rules demanding self-discipline at the highest level.

GOALS MUST BE SPECIFIC. The more detailed we can make the goals, the greater the chance we will reach them. It is mandatory that we write them down and create as many outlined sub-entries as possible.

GOALS MUST BE REALISTIC. Aladdin was *not* a music educator. This routine is futile if we are extreme in either direction: too easy or too difficult. Assess the students' potential, then set the goals one rung higher on the ladder of success.

GOALS MUST MATCH OUR VALUES. If the results of the goal setting are inconsistent with our values, the mind will wipe out the goals much like a computer will erase a document. The plan must be congruent with our purpose in teaching, our purpose in life, and our purposeful being.

VISUALIZE THE GOALS IN DETAIL. Be able to share the vision with the students in a way they understand and see the picture. Enthusiasm and positive energy will always be available when they are clearly aware of their destination. We have all told our students, "Hear the note before you play it" This is merely an extension of that same foolproof advice.

GOALS MUST BE MEASURABLE. If we cannot measure the goals, we cannot chart the progress. Without progress, there is no positive feedback for the mind, and the energy level subsides. Much like a car without gasoline, the goals are without fuel and fall far short of the mark. This is the one flaw which often is carelessly overlooked, but is the necessary component for success.

READ AND REVIEW THE GOALS DAILY. Each time the message is sent to the mind, it reestablishes the forward momentum. Much as a gyroscope keeps a center to an airplane's flight with constant course correction, our mind needs to be fed data to adjust where necessary for goal attainment.

It all sounds so easy. It's not! At least at first, it's not. But like anything else, the habit of doing it time and time again becomes like all other patterns of life. After a given amount of time (twenty-one to twenty-eight days the experts say), goal setting becomes an integral part of our daily routine.

**Good planting means a good harvest.**

**Good habits develop good results.**

Perhaps it is not the will to do good that counts, but rather the will to *prepare* to do good.

We all have the ability for success, but often we allow ourselves to be programmed for failure. After listening to countless people explain why something cannot be accomplished, our subconscious begins to accept this information and we start to behave accordingly. Personal motivation dwindles, and it becomes impossible to define our goals or even explain our plan for reaching the chosen destination. Much like our friend the homing pigeon, we struggle in a hopeless attempt to break out of this professional entrapment. Such an emotional straight jacket, unfortunately, often leads to the proverbial burnout syndrome.

It is *not* a dead-end street. The process of goal setting brings with it an abundance of personal drive. The more vividly we can describe our goals, the more energy is available to us. (Simply recount how the ensemble works with greater intensity just prior to the concert. That goal is easily within sight! Compare that to the lackluster attitude which often occurs immediately after a performance when there might be several weeks before the next goal is at hand.) It has also been demonstrated repeatedly that a disciplined goal-choice will always override a failure-choice in the mind. The choice seems clear!

I recently read a gripping statement of truth which brings all of this to an appropriate end:

**A person who does not improve**
**is no better than a person who cannot improve.**

The goal is to strive for excellence in every facet of our daily lives. Unless we commit to excellence, we are doomed to mediocrity. Why settle for less?

Are we worth our weight in goals?

*"Success is to be measured not so much
by the position that one has reached in life
as by the obstacles which he has overcome
while trying to succeed."*
—Booker T. Washington

# Teaching Life via Music

Another academic year is in full swing, and every music teacher from coast to coast is busy preparing to meet the various performance demands. Whether it is getting the choir ready for the upcoming Rotary banquet or the marching band geared up for the initial half-time spectacular, the race is on!

It is important that we continue to remind ourselves of the countless opportunities we have to teach young people certain truths while we work to improve our musical performances. Music education offers us so many avenues of learning which will make a positive difference in each and every part of the student's life. We have all heard the famous quote: "I hear, I forget. I see, I remember. I do, I understand."

Of course, music involves all of these: hearing, seeing, and most important of all, doing. Therefore, the "education" the students will gain via your class will transfer to each and every part of their lives. It will make an imprint which will help form habits carried throughout each day. Our responsibility demands we extend our level of creativity and offer our best each and every day knowing the impact this very potent learning experience is going to have on the whole being. Quite a challenge! Add to this the musical truth "We're only as strong as the weakest member." Now this kind of situation requires extraordinary teaching—the best!

Each rehearsal or performance affords us the chance to remind the students of the following maxims:

THE VALUE OF COMPETITION IS SELF-IMPROVEMENT. When we compete to "beat" someone, the worth of the process becomes distorted. We compete to gain and grow in our own skills. If we have to win at all costs to feel any self worth, it dictates that someone else must lose. If the judgement call is not in our favor, we might tend to feel worthless, in spite of incredible growth during the preparation process. Even more severe is the fact that we put a limit on our own growth by thinking that winning is the ultimate goal and once we have won, we will no longer need to learn anymore. Music is a constant learning and growing experience. No limits!

FAILURE DOES NOT MEAN INCOMPETENCE. We often tend to equate *failure* with *wrong, bad, lesser, unworthiness, lacking,* etc. In essence, failure is merely an incompletion of the task at hand. It offers us the chance to regroup and seek another solution. In fact, the road to success has many deceptive road signs which lead us to failure and help us get back on course. Music is perfected through a series of failures (e.g., wrong notes, missed key changes, bad counting, unseen accidentals), and the student learns to use these failures as stepping stones to completion. The lesson is simple: The way to become more proficient at anything is to be willing to fail and continue to work on improvement. Of course, this truth applies to each and every part of life. The winners are those who simply do not quit.

INTER-COMMUNICATION IS A MUST. There are many areas of our educational world where students can become totally isolated and receive straight A's without facing any communication with their peers. The communicative skills may be minimal, yet these students are achieving academic honors in all areas. In life, however, we survive based on our ability to work with others in our personal and professional lives. Nobody hides in a musical setting. Everyone counts and the need to communicate is the basis of all quality groups. It is impossible to be in a successful musical organization and not communicate.

MUSIC IS EMOTION. We continue to stress the cognitive side of the learning spectrum. Although we acknowledge the affective domain, we do not dedicate a lot of our school time to this end. As a result, we have high honors students who simply do not feel good about who they are. They are spending a lot of their energy living off the image set by everyone else, and their self-expression is minimal, at best. Music offers a chance to let go and express the rainbow of emotions we all feel, and through this experience expand our own realm of emotional expression. Each student can begin to explore the reality of who they are, what they feel, how they react—living out what is inside of them via the music. Unexpressed emotions serve as the barriers of self-awareness. Inner peace comes from knowing oneself—or as our friend Socrates put it, "Know thyself."

MUSIC IS NOW. Although we prepare for concerts, each rehearsal, in fact, is a concert. It is an "action-experience" and we should treat it as such. Each day we have the chance to create something very unique along our road to success. We are the designers, the architects, the suppliers, the builders, and the decorators. We do it all, and we do it as a living lab. We incorporate mind, body, and spirit. The mind must be sharp to sight-read a chorale, march a half time show, maintain keen attention throughout a forty-five minute orchestral work. The body must be strong and tuned to play a three hour performance in a jazz band, to perform an entire movement to reach new heights of personal/group expression to feel the "groove" in a great swing choir gospel, to trust oneself to soar during the second movement of a beautiful suite, to sense the "oneness" of a woodwind quintet when the communication is beyond words. Music is a human expression of "Now." Life can only be an expression of "Now". All we really have is the moment, the "Now!" Let's teach ourselves and our students to enjoy this gift of "Now."

This list could go on and on, and the fun comes in adding

one's own particular truth(s) to the list. It's so much more than just another subject in school; it is a school within a school.

We have such a privilege to teach in a country where music is part of the daily curriculum. This situation can often cloud our view of reality, and we begin to think music is just another subject. Music is an extension of oneself beyond what *has* to be and into a realm of what *can* be. And we all know, there are no limits to what can be.

As we walk into each rehearsal, it is much like a blank canvas, and the artistic creation of that day will never be duplicated again. Whether it is a tremendous, unforgettable Christmas concert, or the first successful run-through of the B-flat scale by the elementary band, it will live in time as the only one of its kind.

What a challenge, a privilege, a gift, we have each day to teach music through our life...and life through our music. Let the concert begin.

*"That man is a success who has lived well,
laughed often and loved much; who has
gained the respect of intelligent women and
men and the love of children; who never
lacks appreciation of the earth's beauty or
fails to express it; who follows his dreams
and pursues excellence in each task; and
who brings out the best in others, and
gives only the best of himself."*

# A Matter of Excellence

Excellence. It's one of those concepts we talk about
a lot in the performing arts. This group had an excellent
performance. Their show was excellent. That teacher settles
for nothing less than excellence. The behavior of the group was
excellent. The judges thought we had an excellent chance to
qualify for performance bids.

We have all had times in our life when we felt our efforts
were excellent. This is often reflected in what is happening
around us via performances, rehearsals, recruitment, meetings,
workshops and so on. Excellence is usually surrounded with
much activity. Without a busy schedule, we often lose the
sense of excellence which is so important as an acknowledgment
of our efforts. Now, does that mean we have to schedule a score
of events to guarantee excellence? Of course not; however, it
does mean we must be active in our expectations for our
students and in our approach to each and every day in our

teaching profession.

Excellence is not something which is seen on the surface. In fact, it is something quite the opposite of this. Excellence stands for the depth of quality by which a group came out in first place or received a superior rating. Excellence is not based on rankings or ratings. It is not measured by trophies, ribbons, plaques, and awards. Excellence comes from the individual and is generated through an all-out effort to do one's best. If this goal is met, then the rankings or ratings are insignificant as they relate to personal gratification.

At a recent competition, I was visiting with some of the students following their performance. "How did you do?" I asked. "We'll find out tonight at the awards ceremony," answered a young lady. This is a common response and reflects our own insecurity about our individual excellence. Only the performer knows for sure. An adjudicator cannot tell us.

Haven't we all had groups who received the sweepstakes rating, yet certainly did not have an excellent performance? And likewise, we have all experienced those magical moments during a performance, yet did not get our "just" rating. Excellence is a feeling which comes from within. That inner expression of doing one's best!

Excellence produces excellence. We cannot expect it from our students unless we are willing to set the pace via our role modeling as teachers. This puts a tremendous responsibility on each of us, but it also serves as a checkpoint in seeing we do not let down our own standards.

Perhaps it doesn't make any difference if the girl missed a beat. Maybe no one will notice. So what if the officers do not stand with good posture. Maybe the flag routine does not exactly fit the music, but it's pretty close, and the judges are pretty forgiving with most groups. The prop room is a bit out of order, and most of the uniforms are out of date. It's not worth my time to get it organized. (One of the students will probably do it someday.) The list goes on and on, and each rationalization takes us one step away from excellence. If the routine doesn't fit the music, how do you intend to create a drill team excellence for those students? And about the prop room—isn't having one's house in order a fundamental in building excellence?

Quit hiding under your desk! This article is not intended to lay guilt on you. (How do you think I know about all of these shortcomings?) It serves as an opportunity to see how we can improve our own standards of excellence.

There is a tremendous myth which is a part of our profession, and it goes something like this: If I do a good job teaching, everything will fall in place and the program will begin to run itself on self-generated enthusiasm and momentum produced by the participants. They will settle for nothing less than excellence, and I will have the privilege of serving as their director in this utopia of performing arts.

Please step forward if you have achieved this end!

Excellence is not a place of arrival. We don't "get to" excellence. It is a process we go through each and every day. It is a point of departure as well as the journey. It is an unending quest for personal and group achievement. It is the day-by-day, unending practice which is our opportunity to bring all our gifts and talents to fruition to share with others. It is (for those who are ready to hear this) a reflection of our expression of life!

What better contribution could we make to this world than to create excellence for our students? To offer a way of reaching goals which settles for nothing less than the best? To not *follow* the example but rather *set* the example?!

It is not easy, as you well know. It is much easier to sit back and criticize those who risk and fail. It is safer to wait until others have tested the waters before we commit ourselves to anything. However, those who choose this path will never know the thrill of putting it all on the line. That very process is the foundation of excellence.

Maybe you are wondering why anyone would author such material. Did it provoke thought? Excellent! Perhaps you will take a closer look at your own standards of acceptance— *excellent!*

*"Two stonecutter artisans pursuing their craft were observed by travelers passing by. One traveler, seeing the first, remarked on his diligence and effort. 'What is it you are doing?' he asked. 'I'm chipping away at this block of stone,' came the reply. To the second, also hard at work, the traveler posed the same question. "I'm an artist," the craftsman answered, 'I'm building a cathedral.'"*

# Exploring the Seven C's

After ten years of traveling across this country visiting some of our nation's finest high school and college bands, I have discovered certain success patterns that are similar among all of the model programs. Had this whole project started out as a research venture, it could not have been more aptly charted, for the results have proven consistently predictable in every case. Example after example demonstrates there *is* a common architecture for quality bands which is fool-proof, certain to produce excellence in any situation. Yes, *any*.

Before we delve into this formula, the reader can safely bet it is not a "magic formula." Although each model organization I encountered in my travels accomplished their mission(s) with a recipe unique to their situation, the essential ingredient was always countless hours of dedicated investment. There are no shortcuts. If someone is making it look "fast and easy," check behind the curtain; something is not on the up and up.

Many are willing to put in the time. The magic might well be based on *where* the time is invested. Is the focus of the energy producing the best results possible? Are we spending our time wisely? Or are we just treading water, burning up much energy while going nowhere?

It is obvious all the truly outstanding directors have explored the Seven C's, and have garnered a library of knowledge which they faithfully practice in their daily teaching habits. They deal with the same problems, annoyances, inconveniences, and misunderstandings that face all of us, but these common barriers do not divert the forward motion necessary for the growth and development of the given program. Perhaps, after exploring the Seven C's, they realized reaching any destination is possible on the journey to excellence.

## THE SEVEN C'S

COMPETENCE. All master teachers are also master students. They attend workshops, study privately, participate in summer school classes, seek out the leaders in the field and work with them.

The first part of the word indicates the need to "compete." And fine directors do compete—not against one another, but with themselves, constantly raising their standards. Self-improvement is the name of their game. Competence also determines the integrity of the content of the curriculum. Quality in each and every part of the schedule indicates a musical, organizational, and administrative competence in the guidance of the program's destiny, thus reflecting the finest offerings in all facets of the student's school band experience.

Most importantly, these teachers realize that competence is not a point of arrival, but an ongoing process.

COMMITMENT. The common credo is based on a willingness to do whatever needs to be done to achieve excellence. In many cases it appears to be a refusal to accept less than the best and the accompanying attitude which will not allow any kind of permanent failure. Although there may be setbacks along the way, these are used as positive learning experiences. The director regroups with the new data and goes right back into the game with a new plan of action to accomplish the task at hand.

In many instances it means personal sacrifice, last-minute changes in plans, quick adaptation when Murphy's Law prevails, and a constant adjustment to unforeseen circumstances. The outstanding band directors suffer the same problems we all encounter. They are not exempt; they simply refuse to be immobilized by these barriers and often use them as a "teaching lab" to challenge their students' flexibility.

In simple terms their commitment is to do *what needs to be done, when it needs to be done, whether they want to do it or not.* They are committed to *acting* instead of *reacting*.

COMMUNICATION. Being a band director in today's educational system requires a realistic understanding of communication. With the growing importance of band booster organizations, the addition of many extra part time staff members who are teaching lessons, working with various sections, etc., the communication network must be in constant motion to avoid the perils often caused by the proverbial communication gap.

Skillful communication is the lifeblood of any successful organization. The fine directors become adept in the art of presentation, whether it involves a school board member, the executive committee of the parent group, or a scheduling conflict for a student. Both verbal and written communication become an ongoing top priority and not a casual afterthought.

Most importantly, these directors are keenly aware that music and communication are one and the same. Just as one can never be totally satisfied or ever attain musical perfection, so it is with communication. Since many aspects of the program are dependent upon various support people and groups, the more skilled the director is in the communicative nuances, the better the opportunities brought to the student musicians.

CONFIDENCE. Although this is often difficult to put into definitive terms, we all know the satisfaction of being led by someone who is comfortable with the responsibilities at hand. Unfortunately, we all know the uneasiness of dealing with someone who is insecure and unstable, not to mention irresponsible.

Certainly, years in the ranks (maturity) bring about a sense of confidence, but that is only one small aspect of the atmosphere that is created by a confident director. In many ways, it is a culmination of everything we have addressed up to this point in our exploration of the Seven C's. Confidence is that inner sense of knowing what to do, when to do it, what deserves attention and what does not, a steadiness and calmness in making decisions, a non-emotional problem-solving logic which benefits everyone. Perhaps it is the antithesis of the typically described artist's moody personality.

Ultimately, these confident directors are quick to admit if they have erred in judgement, and refuse to let their ego get in the way of the welfare of the band. Those who are truly confident admit they can be wrong. Honesty is still the most respected of all human traits.

CONSIDERATION. One of the reasons these fine educators continue to succeed centers around their personality and the fact they are considerate. Although firm in their demands, they are not inflexible at the expense of the students' musical experience. There is a constant reshaping of program requirements to accommodate work schedules, conflicts with other school events, testing requirements, and unexpected, irreversible family responsibilities.

This sense of fairness seems to bring with it the ability to distinguish between a student's legitimate explanation of a short-coming and a fabricated excuse. The attribute of consideration is mirrored by those around this exemplary director, and the common discipline problems which plague many programs are non-existent.

This certainly does not indicate a lack of personal demand or discipline. Quite the contrary; these standards require complete dedication to the program, and a dogmatic, all-or-nothing approach gives way to a realistic understanding of today's fast-paced society and the need to work within that framework, not against it.

Consideration could well be the oil which eliminates "friction" in efficiently running a fine band program. Judicious application is the key.

CONCENTRATION. This might better be viewed as the ability to shift one's thinking at a moment's notice and apply total concentration to a certain area of concern.

As much as every keen director attempts to schedule each day to allow appropriate time for score study, staff meetings, correspondence, planning, student updates, and so on, we all know the unfavorable odds of it all falling into place with ease. Dealing with countless unknowns is simply a given. It is naive to think that one's projected plan for the day will be fulfilled without some interruptions or delays. The ability to reshift one's thinking to accommodate whatever surfaces demands a phenomenal amount of concentration.

The number of professional hats worn by today's band director requires a continual reacclamation to constantly shifting responsibilities. Immediate concentration is an absolute requirement, for the pace does not allow the luxury of a detailed preparation at each change of focus, nor can one afford to make a half-hearted effort which could well affect/influence a decision of major consequences.

There simply is no substitute for the alert mind, always cognizant of the present situation and ready to adjust at all times.

COOPERATION. With the exception of competence, this might well be the most valuable of all the Seven C's. It is more than getting along with others. It extends into the realm of outreaching attitudes and opinions, program themes, organizational goals, rehearsal environment, expected and accepted behavioral patterns.

The distinction between a good program and a great program hinges on this quality. In talking with the students, it is apparent they are supportive of all organizations in the school, and neighboring school bands. Their self-worth is not built on comparison, but rather highlighted by their sense of cooperation. A unified appreciation for the efforts of others is obviously achieved via the director's constant reminders of an open-minded approach to evaluation rather than an "either/or" concept.

Other area directors speak highly of the cooperative efforts of these model directors sensing a non-judgmental attitude of mutual support. A genuine caring and sharing is always the dominant theme wrapped in an open-door policy of willingness to help upon request.

The whole program is a class act living the treasury of understanding discovered while exploring the Seven C's.

Final page of the navigator's log....

It all appears to be so neatly packaged, a certain map of professional success. Of course this is not the case. The tried and true band director knows the search for excellence is a life-long journey. Each of the Seven C's could be a study within itself. This brief survey is only one piece of the giant puzzle which should tickle the reader's curiosity to continue the pursuit: to faithfully study those proven music educators and understand the realistic concepts put into practice each and every day which produce successful results.

There is no doubt in my mind that my own travels will continue to offer many new insights into the countless extensions of the Seven C's. Our swiftly changing society is constantly challenging us to come up with new innovations in recruiting, retention, scheduling, and a host of other survival responsibilities. We owe it to our programs, our students, and ourselves to "set sail" and devote our energies to a constant exploration of positive ways to insure the growth and development of our bands. Ahoy!

---

This article first appeared in slightly different form in "BD Guide."

*The rung of a ladder was never meant*
*to rest upon, but only to hold a man's*
*foot long enough to enable him to*
*put the other somewhat higher.*
                                    *—Thomas Huxley*

# The Key to
# Success in Teaching:
# The Demand for Excellence

Everyone wants "the answer"—the answer to everything from installing a garage door opener to dealing with an irate parent. If I just had "the answer," all of my problems would be gone. Peace, freedom from worry, and ecstasy would prevail every moment of every day!

Where does one find "the answer"?

As we look around, it is obvious we all seek this fantastic information, and we all seem to go about it via various avenues: more education, yoga, conference calling, self-abuse, marriage, divorce, remarriage, vegetarian diets, mystic brew, emotional bruises, physical health programs, sun tan beds, and R-O-L-A-I-D-S. How do *you* spell *relief?*

What does it take to bring us to this wonderful, safe land of success and self-satisfaction?

For everyone who is looking for the "foolproof, absolutely

guaranteed, will-never-fail secret," this is not the article for you—head back to the sun tan beds! This message is for the person who is dedicated to this great profession called teaching. This is for the educator who stumbles and falls, makes mistakes—like locking the keys in the car, worrying when a student expresses personal problems, and not being able to find the needed insurance papers or the hospital when an ankle is broken during the faculty volleyball game. Maybe this is you!

Our job as teachers has been scribed, prescribed, and described to the point we may not know what we're supposed to do. In spite of all this illusion, confusion, delusion about the institution, we know we are counting on ourselves to be successful at our chosen field of endeavor, and the reflection of our efforts can be seen in our students day in and day out. This observation and evaluation serves as the fuel for our forward progress as well as the "emotional breaks" of self-doubt. We all know the students can make or break our day, and the reality is they reflect our own attitude. Therefore, it is of ultimate importance we institute a high feeling of self-worth in our students and colleagues so we can enjoy this reflection of attitudes.

The one, absolute, obvious quality of every great teacher is the ability to communicate the importance of self-discipline in their students. They can focus the energy, and as a result, accomplishment jumps to a new level. This creates a greater desire to succeed, and the self-discipline goes up accordingly. It sounds simple, but the really fine teachers know the process is far more complicated. Focusing the energy is an art! What "turns on" one student may "turn off" the next. The very key to opening the lock to a student's unlimited potential may be magically effective on Monday and totally useless on Tuesday. The number of variables which control this phenomenon are infinite, not to mention the changes you, as an educator, go through each day which also affect your perspective. So what's "the answer"?

It seems the successful people in the teaching world share one commonality: the demand for excellence—and they insist on, and demonstrate their own, persistence in this quest. In common terms, They don't quit 'til they get it right! They all have their own ways of handling their organizational procedures, they use all different kinds of support materials, they may violate every rule in the book, and they may project every attitude associated with "bad teaching," but they succeed time after time. Students will go the extra mile for them ninety percent of the time—and whatever it takes, they somehow seem to meet the call.

Self-discipline produces a feeling of self-worth which generates a higher level of self-discipline, etc., etc., etc. This all leads to a feeling of self-esteem, and since our feelings control our behavior, it stands to reason that someone with high self-esteem is going to behave and perform with a success-oriented focus. The result is success.

Again, it sounds so simple; just work hard...feel good about yourself...and work harder so you can feel even better! Every self-help book will give you that recipe, and you'll put down the book and be ready to move mountains. However,...

Here's the part they forgot to mention: Let's work hard...and then *fail* at our task—do we still feel good? *No!* In this case, hard work produced a negative feeling. The logical mind quickly says: Do I feel good, or do I feel worse? This is exactly where the break comes between those who make it and those who don't. Most people can rationalize "not doing" almost anything. If we do nothing, we never have to suffer the penalties (the feelings) of failure. We can also stand back and point to where others have failed and brag on being "exempt" because we knew better than to try it in the first place. Sad, but true!

It is at this juncture we make the choice for failure or success. The "failure" of the task can be corrected, but if we quit, we're done! The mind will struggle internally, If you go again and fail, then you'll be twice as bad! (Do I dare take the chance of feeling twice as bad?!) "The answer": Learn from the failure and go right back into the task again. Tackle it from a different angle, get the help of some other people, research another way to go about it, break it down into smaller parts, but don't quit! The importance of the task may be inconsequential, but the feeling you establish is going to be the groundwork for the next problem you face. Simply don't allow feelings of failure to be a part of your thinking pattern. The joy of breakthrough accomplishment is so tremendous that it almost justifies whatever the price one must pay.

The bonus of never quitting (as a teacher) comes from the

role model we set for the many students who are watching us with more learning awareness than most of us want to admit. They see that you, too, run up against obstacles which seem overwhelming, that even teachers don't have the answers, but must search and risk. The feelings of inferiority which dominate the young people's thinking are then evident in our behavior; however, we model for the youth what to do with these feelings: Go on in spite of them!

The habits and patterns which are being ingrained during the school years will determine the patterns of life. Although we always instruct, "Grow up...Be mature...Quit acting like a child...Come on, grow up!"—do *we* ever grow up? Sometimes we imply that when one is "grown-up" all the problems of life will have the answers at hand, and we will simply live in bliss and happiness. We all know growing up is going to be a process until death. With that in mind, what an opportunity we have in front of us every day to teach, taking the problems of life and turning them into living examples of learning experience. Each day becomes a lab class of how to handle this wonderful thing called *life!*

One of the greatest benefits which comes from the demand for excellence is the understood rule that you can't quit until you have achieved. There is no room for anything less. Do we dare ask anything less of our students? Of ourselves?

It is a proven statistic that we have six to eight failures for every one success. Knowing that, how could we possibly stop after four, five, or even six bad attempts? The payoff could easily be in the next try. When we fall down, it is so easy to lay there and defend why we cannot get back up, but that only supports the failure. Any truly successful person will tell you the temptation to "stay down" never leaves—the mind seems to always throw the temptation right in our face: Stay down. Don't take any more stupid chances. Everyone else is down, too. You aren't good enough—you'll fall again. People are laughing at you. Who do you think you are anyway?

When this happens, immediately begin to talk to yourself. What made me fall? Where did it hurt? What could I have done differently? Is there anything I can use in this experience to help if I fall again? What's the best way to get up? This very technique of "self-talk" may be the one key factor in establishing a high level of self-discipline. It's a matter of serving as your own cheerleader—focus your own energy and demand excellence from yourself.

As teachers, we must do this for ourselves, but we can also serve as the "surrogate cheerleader" for the students. When we see them fall (fail), we must jump right up and urge them to give it another shot. It is the chance for us to encourage, to give new information, to express feelings, to strengthen our resistance, to teach. Failure is not bad. We must welcome these instances and focus the energy of the circumstance so we can prepare for the next level. Through all of this effort, we learn, we grow, we expand—and then we can pass that knowledge right back to the students.

In conclusion, the demand for excellence is seen around us every day. Each person interprets this quality, this attribute, in many ways: some with strict rules, some through expressive sharing, some through group dynamics, and many through a combination of all these methods, plus many more. Whatever it takes, the obvious striving for excellence is always predominant. Wonderful teachers just don't quit...and their students mirror this quality. Maybe the students never reach the top of the mountain, but they sure have a magnificent learning experience on the way up!

The answer? Don't quit! The way not to quit? Don't quit! And when you can justify quitting in every logical way: Don't quit! And when you're tired and you feel like nobody really cares: Don't quit! And when all else fails, take R-O-L-A-I-D-S, then get back to work—you're setting the pace for all of us!

*"If you blame others for your failures,
do you credit them with your success?"*

# A Straight-A's Curriculum for Success

Our traditional grading system suggests that getting straight A's is the ultimate goal of the successful student. We have all played the game with fervor—cramming before the final exam, spending late hours with study groups, forcing down that final cup of coffee with the test notes strategically placed beside the cup, and focusing every bit of mental, emotional, and physical energy on the cherished "A" which will guarantee our success as one of today's music educators. Yet we all know this doesn't always prove true. The top of the class doesn't always prove to be the front-runners in the profession. There are countless stories concerning the brilliant and talented college music major who found the rehearsal room to be a less-than-desirable environment, and who subsequently chose a career in a totally unrelated area. On the other hand, we well remember the student who completed all the required work, but never seemed to be on the cutting edge—and now they are responsible for a model music program which stands as an example of excellence in your region. How can this be explained?

Perhaps there is another level of getting straight A's we often do not see. Maybe there is more to it than the memorization of material and the ability to test well. Let's assume there are several required courses which are not in the catalog, but woven into the context of the learning experience. The final grades do not show up on the transcript at the end of the semester, but they are well-recorded in the minds and hearts of our colleagues and friends.

How well are we doing in these tuition-free, prerequisite-for-success classes in human relations?

ACCEPTANCE 101. This core class is a must for the educator who will be working with students from different socioeconomic backgrounds, or multireligious affiliations. If members of the group have different opinions or personal tastes, this information is necessary in creating a working, productive community. The fundamental theme of Acceptance 101 centers on the ability to withhold judgement and see everyone as having worth simply because they are part of the organization.

APPRECIATION 100-Ph.D. Students at any level can enroll in this class. It can be repeated for credit anytime and is often recommended as a refresher course for the aspiring graduate enrollee. The information is not particularly difficult to absorb, but it seems to be easily forgotten in the crises of everyday life. Highly recommended for anyone suffering from a cynical view of the profession. Much of the course work requires out of class participation.

AFFABILITY 400. Although this is an upper-level offering, anyone is eligible to enroll. Formerly titled Cooperation 400, the emphasis deals with the premise that the ability to get along with others is the single most important commodity of our profession. Eighty-five percent of all problems are people related. The research revealed will help clear up many of the daily problems caused by personality conflicts. (A prerequisite class for PROFESSION SUCCESS—HONORS CLASS.)

ACKNOWLEDGMENT 201. Giving credit where credit is due serves as the entire syllabus for this course and demonstrates the positive effects of supporting the behavior of those who are contributing and showing dedication to the goal. It is suggested that you do not sign up for this offering until you have completed ACCEPTANCE 101 and APPRECIATION 100.

ACCOUNTABILITY 000-LIFETIME. The "ability to be accountable" is the sister course of RESPONSIBILITY—"the ability to respond." Students who complete this class will learn to avoid blame and revenge in their professional and personal lives. They will learn the art of completion. Task completion is the number one builder of positive self-image, and personal success is in direct proportion to task completion.

We might entitle that unwritten page in the catalogue "Secrets to Effective Human Relations." The faculty for these classes are the people whom we are with each day. Our grades are posted in the thoughts, conversations, body language, and general behavior of those around us. If we are not satisfied with the results of our efforts, it should be clear that we need to alter our contribution to the classroom of life.

When evaluating ourselves and others, let's not forget the importance of getting straight A's at every level. The curriculum outlined in this article is one we must study and practice every moment of every day. The agenda of self-improvement must be become a habit of life. We all have so much to learn; we will be students forever. A person who does not improve is no better than someone who cannot improve. Let's dedicate ourselves to getting straight A's.

*"To lead a symphony, one must
sometimes turn his back on the crowd."*

# Music Education:
# Job or Mission?!

It is called music education—a profession which demands at least a four year stint in college, followed by a second,
and sometimes a third, higher degree, not to mention the
countless workshops, conventions, seminars, and clinics which
are vital if one is to maintain any sense of "being current" in
the field. Once qualified, the employee (teacher) is given the
opportunity to start at the bottom rung of the salary ladder,
regardless of talent-level, success in the academic world,
previous accomplishments, or how many gold stars you received
during beginning piano lessons. It's called pay scale.

Once the position is obtained, the revenue increase in no
way reflects the level of productivity, success, or growth of
the program. There is no overtime pay, vacation compensation,
travel allowance, expense account, or Christmas bonus plans.
Clothing allotments are rare also. This position has no business
hours; instead, the employee is asked to "do whatever it takes"
to complete the endless task at hand. If it requires evenings,
weekends, holidays, or altering family plans, it becomes a
"silent understanding" as part of the initial contract.

Although class size is a major issue for many teachers, the music educator is encouraged to get as many people as possible. School mandates limiting classrooms to a maximum of twenty-six students are overlooked when it comes to the 175-member band. State per capita budgetary laws do not seem to apply. In fact, the music educator is expected to "fund-raise" to create enough revenue to support the suggested overload of students.

With increased academic requirements, it is assumed this skilled artist will be able to embellish the present program, even though rehearsal time has been cut and schedules have been altered to accommodate everything from "Advanced Computer Repair" to "Latin IV" (the newest requirement for college admission). And yet, the music educator moves forward, dauntless in the pursuit of giving music to those students who, like the teacher, are determined to fulfill their need for this magnificent art. And they say it's not a mission.

The monetary compensation is absurd when one considers the number of hours these great teachers give day in and day out. It's not even minimum wage. The "free time" which accompanies this particular vocation is spent listening to musical groups, traveling to hear musical performances, vacationing where there are music festivals, signing up for clinics about music, and listening to promotional records. The free time is a way to find more work time—a chance to research more, to create more knowledge, to find more ways to bring a greater learning experience back to the students.

This is not a sacrifice, but the result of a personal choice to live life with this kind of focus, to make the musical experience as positive as possible for those young people who have decided to dedicate time and effort to "learning music."

It is not a matter of right or wrong, but a matter of choice. When the issue of fairness comes into play, the music educator is out of the ball park before the game ever starts. There is so much more to this profession than meets the eye.

It is crucial for the music educator to be able, at times, to transcend personal wants and become totally engaged in the "serving of people."

The music educator must get past "what is good for me," and focus on what will be good for others.

We feel the greatest satisfaction and purpose in life when

we help improve the quality of life for others. It has nothing to do with self-denial or thinking of others as more important than self. It is a level of living far beyond that. A music educator who is vitally involved in his/her work is literally a part of the purpose. There is no focus on what one does to get attention, or even a major concern about what others will think of the action. This dedicated individual moves forward on target because there is a great satisfaction and happiness in being so determined. External rewards and opinions of others really are of no interest.

The real music educator is excited about the activities and completely involved in the action every day, regardless of what it is, knowing that the work is making the world a better place for at least one human being.

It is a mission! Yes, many people will disagree; however, those are the ones still trying to make the profession fit in the box like other professions. It's an entirely different language based on a sense of "inner knowing" about what has to be done and having the right talents and the given desire to do it. The "payoffs" far exceed the new car, new house, lake cottage, or similar personal "prerequisites." There simply is no price tag on the glow that can be seen in a young person's eyes, or from a group of students when they sense the communication level available to them via music—a whole new language of sharing.

So much of what we read is "pragmatic" information. This is very valuable, but now and then we should press ourselves just a bit to look within and really remind ourselves why we chose music as a way of life. Without that basic understanding, all the pragmatic information will be of little use.

As Carl Jung so brilliantly stated, "From the beginning I had a sense of destiny, as though my life was assigned to me by fate and had to be fulfilled. This gave me an inner security, and, though I could never prove it to myself, it proved itself to me. I did not have this certainty, it had me."

Perhaps we will never explain it, nor understand it, but we will continue to live it and to bring it to those who can share in this tremendous learning experience. Those who have the gift are certainly a chosen few. The next time you feel like throwing in the towel because of some irritated parent, upset student, inflexible administrator, or pushy salesman, just remember your mission. Ours is a task of cutting the weeds so the students can get through. Sharpen the blade and jump back in the jungle. We need you!

Now is the time. Welcome aboard!

*"There are no limits to the amount
of good you can accomplish if you
don't care who gets the credit."*

# Student Behavior:
# Fact, not Fiction

Band director? Psychologist? Music teacher? Counselor? Performer? Confidant? And other assorted job-related responsibilities included in the profession!

How many psychology courses did you take in college? Do you ever feel you're facing a problem with a student that is beyond your expertise in relationship to counseling or guidance for the student's well being? Is most of your time spent teaching music, or do you find yourself spending all of your time handling various situations within the environment just to keep the program afloat?

We are never totally prepared for what faces us as teachers, and when we are confronted with the reality of the educational world, it can be a frightening, frustrating, confusing, and discouraging set of experiences. Many things you are asked to do as a music educator are well beyond your expertise (i.e., disciplinary action, emotional unrests). The instinctive behavior is to scream, Foul! The truth is, right or wrong, prepared or not prepared, you will face such circumstances. So rather than waste nonproductive energy on whether it's "fair" or not, let's assume a positive posture and begin to seek information on how to deal with the problems at hand. Act instead of react, and shift from merely existing to creative growth, where we can examine and solve problems.

Nice words, but how does this ideological fairyland become a reality? To begin with, we must acknowledge some of the things going on for young people in today's teenage world. You may not like all of this data, but to dismiss it is setting yourself up for certain failure in your teaching career. When we understand and learn about the behavior patterns of youth, then (and only then) can we begin to work with them, not in spite of them.

Do you remember your first *real* day of teaching music? How excited you were to impart all of your knowledge into those thirsty little minds. Remember your visions of all the students waiting in eager anticipation of every word of wisdom you were going to share with them? More fairyland. Rarely does it happen that way, or even come close to it, because we have been working under the false assumption the students will be filled with a tremendous desire to learn. A dangerous, as well as inaccurate, deduction. Successful teachers are those people who accept the reality of the situation at hand and move forward from that point. They have a grip on where the students are coming from and are assertive in the necessity to go to them instead of waiting for the students to magically "come of age."

We all need to see that teenagers are facing a higher degree of stress than ever before. Their lives are full of pressures which not only dictate their daily behavior, but cause them to make choices which are in need of adult counterbalance. Whether we agree about our own need to handle this added responsibility (on the teacher's part) or not, isn't the question—you will handle it; you have no choice. How to handle it is the question. Playing B-flat in tune is important, but if the child behind the instrument is dealing with: a broken home, extended pressure to make grades to qualify for a certain college, drug or alcohol abuse, emotional crisis with friends, trying to work and go to school at the same time, etc.—then you can correct the technical part of the problem, but you still have the problem. Next time B-flat appears, guess what?!

Too often, we react to this particular situation by overreacting. Venting anger, embarrassing the student, espousing "Lecture 26" to the entire group, or whatever, will not solve the problem. The problem is not that the student doesn't want to play B-flat in tune; it's that the student is so preoccupied with a stressful situation (regardless of when it happened) that he or she isn't even aware of the out-of-tune note. Sometimes the student isn't even in the room...so to speak! The immediate, and all-too-common, response is, "Well, they shouldn't drag their feelings into the rehearsal and ruin it for everyone else!" None of us should! But we do, and we must deal with what is, not what should be!

The next time you stand in front of your group, remember these facts about the teenagers of today:

• Sixty-five percent of 13-year-olds have experimented with alcohol. One out of every five consumes a measurable amount of liquor at least once a week.

• Sixty-four percent of teens have experienced drugs prior to graduation.

• Teenage suicide rate has increased 131 percent since 1975. It's the third leading cause of death among today's youth— and for every successful suicide, there are fifty attempts!

• Exposure to explicit adult sexual behavior is more accessible than ever in our society: cable TV adult channels, less censorship restrictions on free TV, growth in the number of adult bookstores, etc. By age 19, seventy percent of the students have been involved in a full-scale premarital relationship.

• Just over twenty percent of the students are living in a home with only one biological parent. These students are adjusting their lives to fit their circumstances.

These are just a few of the shocking statistics available when one researches the present status of the teenage lifestyle. It's not the purpose of this article to judge whether the above facts are right or wrong, but merely to inform you: This is the way it is. The point is, you can quickly see what kind of stress, or pressure, exists in our schools. They have become a microcosm

of the adult world and the trend of growing up q
brought with it all the emotional hazards and ailmε
adult world. We simply can't ignore these issues; they
and we must adjust our teaching techniques to deal wi,
or the B-flat will never be in tune...nor will the studer
will you!

What can I do? How can I help? In what direction do I go?
Once we begin to face the situation with a clear understanding,
we have won half the battle. Sidestepping the issues is simply
adding fuel to the present fire. If you've made it this far in the
article, you have taken a big step. The following suggestions
will serve as guidelines. There is no answer which will solve
every problem, because every problem is unique to that situation.
This information will give you some idea of where your energy
will be best spent.

DON'T TRY TO TURN THE CLOCK BACK. Too many
people want to return to the "good old days." While they are
verbalizing about how great things used to be, the excellent
teachers are dealing with the present and preparing for the
future. Update!

EXPRESS YOUR CARE FOR STUDENTS BY SAYING NO!
Young people need help in decision making. Teach the value
of giving up the short-term instant gratification in exchange
for the long-term goal...and that the enjoyment comes via the
journey, or focus. Learning to deal with "No" can be the most
meaningful tool you can share with them.

IN EVERY DECISION, DEAL WITH THE PRINCIPLE,
NOT THE PRESSURE. Young people have learned the game
of manipulation very well from the adult world, and you can
easily get conned into doing something which is in complete
opposition to what would be most beneficial to the program.
When the students understand your thinking is always based
on what is best for them in the overall scheme of things, they
will begin to respect your decision making. You must be honest
with your own integrity. You won't always be popular, but you
will be a great role model for everyone!

TEACH PERSISTENCE BY BEING PERSISTENT. Learning

57

example is still the most effective method. If your students observe you tackling the problems of the day with a positive approach, they are likely to copy or mirror your behavior when they are around you. Beware: the reverse of this is also true when applied to negative example. A great friend once told me he could predict the performance of any group by spending ten minutes with the director in his or her office. His theory was amazingly accurate. Persistence is an absolute must in musical growth. Demonstrate how to stretch and grow through expanding your limits. Be an effective mirror source.

DEAL WITH THE CONFRONTING ISSUES IMMEDIATELY AND PRIVATELY. Although discipline problems and irritating happenings invite the intimidation "sledgehammer," the "instant resolution" technique will come back to haunt you. Whenever we embarrass someone into behaving or seeing it our way, the problem will silently snowball and appear with much more intensity than the original issue. Get it out in the open and clean it up!

ENCOURAGE COMMUNICATION AT ALL LEVELS. When you find some divisions in the organization and a "coldness" about individuals, sections, or various groups set in, it is much like the calm before the storm. The only way to offset the problem is with communication. Share what is going on with your students, your colleagues, your administration—everyone who touches your life. Communication is a learned habit, and it must be practiced. Set the example!

BE CALM AND LOGICAL. Students are looking for some stability. In the extreme emotions which make up a good part of teenage growth patterns, (the do-or-die situations), it is so important they have an offsetting personality. This counter-balance in life could be your most important contribution to their lives.

HAVE A SENSE OF HUMOR—LIGHTEN UP! Too often, we extend far too much anxiety towards a problem. Take care of it and move on. Learn to be "glad" right after you're "mad." Stick to you guns, and don't let any negative emotion drag through the entire day. Only in traumatic experiences does trauma have any real value. Teenagers need to see that life doesn't have to be lived at the emotional pace of their favorite soap opera.

Now, let's return to square one.

None of us took enough psychology courses to give us all the answers. The answers lie within the personal research we do each day.

If you feel inadequate about handling some of the student's emotional upset, welcome aboard! Simply take it one step at a time and express care every step of the way.

So you're not teaching music every minute of the day. Who is? The question is, Are you *teaching* every minute of the day? Remember to include yourself as one of your students!

The B-flat scale is important, but far more important is the understanding of *why* the B-flat is important! There is no use straightening the lamp shade if the house is burning down. Or, as one very wise teacher once told me, "Use the music to make your students, not the students to make your music!" Bull's-eye!

*"A diamond is a piece of
coal that stuck to the job."*

# Press On

W hat does it take to be a success in the world of music education?

Remember when your college professor stood in front of the students enrolled in Teaching Methods 101 and asked this very question? Then after a moment of serious pondering, the hands began to raise, and the wisdom of the class was transferred to the blackboard. The obvious answer came first—musicianship!

"Absolutely!" confirmed Dr. Noteworthy. "You won't go far in this profession unless you have a mastery of your art. Your musical talents must be polished, and there should be a lifetime commitment to the study of this vast field of knowledge."

"Organization. Every great music teacher I know is extremely organized," stated Perry Perfect as he wiped some dust from his wing-tip shoes.

"Ah, yes! It's important to remember many fine musicians have failed as music educators due to their lack of ability to organize the countless tasks which were before them. Good thinking, Mr. Perfect."

"Leadership. What good will it do to be a fine, organized musician unless the person has some leadership skills? Just look within our own School of Music—the best performing groups are the organizations with the strongest leaders. Don't you agree?" asked Farah Flawless.

"I do agree," confirmed Professor "N" with a smile. "And by the way, let's all make sure we get out and vote for Miss Flawless in our upcoming student government election. It will be a real step forward for our music programs to have this kind of representation. Thank you again, Farah."

And the class continued to share their ideas about the qualities of an outstanding music educator, hoping the magic formula would appear and insure their futures in this exciting profession. The blackboard was filled as the class ran out of time and there were headings, sub-headings, Roman numerals, parenthesis, etc.: personality, charisma, education, research, communicative skills, political understanding, commitment, desire, loyalty, personal health, sensitivity. (Yes, even "ability to fund-raise" made it on the board!)

We all have those notebooks tucked away safely in our basements or sitting proudly on our office shelves. When any student comes in and announces they are going to seek a career in music education, we promptly recall the list of qualities (with our own attributes at the top of the list) and have a "heart to heart" about the reality of what lies ahead of them.

What if we had to condense all of this into one, absolute, certain quality which every successful music educator possesses? Every quality "on the board" or "in the notebook" is a *must*, but perhaps we have put the cart slightly ahead of the horse. The "list" almost suggests we are born with these attributes. You have heard it said countless times, "She's a born musician. He's a born leader. She was born with inherent organizational skills." We all know better. The successful people in this field may have certain strengths, but the one commonality is their ability to work. They simply put their nose to the grindstone, day in and day out, and their level of production mirrors their amount of investment. Without this fundamental absolute, the rest of the list is not valid. In other words, it is not just the quality we are discussing but the implementation of the quality! What does it take to implement?

Everyone can talk about the most outstanding music educator they know, and the reasons for success of those educators are: fine administrative support, good rehearsal facilities, great parental organization, a wonderful library, a superb feeder program, and so on. And all those reasons are true—but back up one step: Where did all of that come from? Who is responsible for developing the relationship with the administrators, designing and promoting the need for good facilities, creating and nurturing the parent group, purchasing and organizing the library, working hand in hand with the feeder program? Of course, the reason for success is all the apparent strengths we see in front of us, but how did these strengths get to be strengths? Hereinafter lies the answer.

All the top-notch people seem to have this desire for excellence which is unwavering. They focus on a goal and are willing to pay the price for achievement of that goal. Their predictable success at everything is a given. They simply will not give up; they are willing to "take their lumps" and continue the quest. As a result of this energy, we label their success with various "reasons for" such as: great leadership, fine organization, strong musical talent, and so on. Notice these labels came *after* they have attained a level of recognition. Nobody paid a lot of attention to them when the organization started with fourteen members, the rehearsal room was a converted storage basement, and the booster group was nonexistent. Now, after three years of talking to students in the hallway, serving as sponsor for the junior varsity softball club, sweeping coal dust from the rehearsal room floor, and eating stale cookies at Mrs. Potential-Booster's home, the group is performing at the state convention. And now, following the fine performance, we speculate on why the band/choir/orchestra is excellent. The same reasons prevail. The success is based on one dominant theme: persistence—the ability to continue regardless of the barriers which stand between the music educator and the goal.

Take, for example, a program of national acclaim in which students are born with perfect pitch, the entire community sees the music program as the answer to positive child rearing, invitations from throughout the world to perform are a daily occurrence, and the Eastern School of Music recruits directly from the top groups—assuming the students haven't already accepted a major European tour or a recording contract. Then the director leaves to take on a new challenge, and applications from everywhere flood into the administration office. What a plum position! This job has it all! In comes the new director who has credentials equal to a saint. Demands are met for paneling and carpeting the office, rescheduling the curriculum, buying new equipment, and generally meeting every request of Mr. or Ms. Right. Everything is going great guns until the daily grind begins. Reality hits: Students begin to drop out of the program, a noticeable lack of musicianship is evident at the concerts, new administrative restrictions appear, attendance at parent meetings drops, nobody answers the phone in the music office, last-minute time changes for rehearsals and concerts become frequent, communication with parents about schedules and time frames wanes, there is a slump in the attitude of the students in the program. Why is it different? What has gone awry? We can look to see which of the qualities on the "list" are not a part of the new director's repertoire, or we can immediately look at the persistence level demonstrated by the new leader.

In the meantime, the former director, who is now at a nearby school, has turned the new school's program in a positive direction within a matter of weeks. The students begin to glow and have the same sense of forward motion which was the "reason for success" in the first set-up. And soon Program B is miles ahead of Program A. The reason: persistence on the part of the director.

We have come to think that persistence means an unlimited investment of time, and that simply isn't so. Quality persistence is far more valuable than quantity persistence. Once there is the established determination to attain the goal, then the list of qualities comes into play. One must work smart! The common complaint "I have been at school since 6:00 A.M. and won't get to leave here until 11:30 P.M. tonight!" would lead us to think the person has really put in a full day and has a lot of persistence. The next conclusion would be "They probably got a lot of work done." This is a "time trap" which is easy to fall into. Are the free hours spent doing productive, priority work, or simply used in time-filler ways? Could any of the chores at hand be accomplished by a sharp student staff? Are there things to be done which are being put off until another time? What teaching outside of the class has gone on through the day? What are we getting out of the investment of our day (our lives) and how is the investment going to pay off tomorrow? The successful people send everything through this filter of thinking. Their time is used wisely, and they refuse to waste their precious day because they realize they will never get it back. They operate on quality persistence at all times—personally, professionally, emotionally, and spiritually. They understand this is not the dress rehearsal; rather, this is it!

This quality persistence leads them to constantly evaluate themselves, both strengths and weaknesses. They use their strengths in a positive, supportive way and spend time and effort doing whatever is necessary to improve where they are weak. In many cases, they find ways to substitute for whatever they are lacking. (Perhaps this means bringing in another teacher or college students, taking extra classes, etc.) The point is they admit weaknesses and don't try to cover them. They expose their students to the best people they can find and are always searching for different ways to find new growth experiences for the program.

The really successful people never arrive, but are enjoying the journey of new experiences in learning. Although they are satisfied with their accomplishments, they never rest on their laurels—they use their successes as stepping stones to the next level of excellence. They almost invite risks and are thrilled at the chance to accept the new. They see failure as a chance to rework an idea and make it better, and they look at every problem as an opportunity to improve. They never waste energy whining about "what isn't," but immediately begin to look at "what can be." They turn "blame energy" into "how-can-we-fix-it" energy. Their persistence is ultimate in support of the goal.

This wisdom of our many great leaders has been passed down from generation to generation, and these truths (which they saw then) are still catalysts to those people who are success-bound today. One such truth continues to appear on many office walls, desk plaques, the backs of business cards, and inside fortune cookies. It gives us the secret to what it takes to be a success in music education:

## Press On

Nothing in the world can take the place of persistence. Talent will not; nothing is more common than unsuccessful people with talent. Genius will not; unrewarding genius is almost a proverb. Education will not; the world is full of educated derelicts. Persistence and determination alone are omnipotent.

*—Calvin Coolidge*

Our quality list is only valid when built on the foundation of persistence. There is no "free lunch." There will be a few lucky breaks along the way, but even those have been created by a set of circumstances built on many hours of investment. To succeed, we cannot depend on the luck of the draw, the stars being in the right order, the principal being a former trombone player, or the students being weaned on Mozart. Succeeding is a simple matter of accepting what is and moving forward from that point. Those who make it to the top of the mountain will find it to be treacherous, scary, demanding, disappointing, and exhausting—but it will also be thrilling, strengthening, awakening, caring, and, most of all, a chance to offer young people the wonderful experience of growth via music.

"Are you *willing* to be successful?" *not*, "Do you *want* to be successful?" We all have the "list." Who will put it into action?!

Thomas Edison said, "Genius is just perseverance in disguise."

When we can "role model" this quality of persistence, the very best teaching in our career is happening. The "short cut" is the "long cut." What a great opportunity to serve others by way of our gift of music. Press on!

*"Our chief want in life is somebody
who will make us do what we can."*
— *Ralph Waldo Emerson*

# The Real Key
# to Successful Motivation

How many times have we all heard the helpless statement, "I just can't seem to motivate my students?" That is absolutely the truth! Nobody can motivate another person. We can manipulate, coerce, inspire, urge, threaten, beg, demand, command, plea, order, instruct—but we cannot motivate them. Motivation is, at all times, an individual choice. Knowing this, we can quickly deduct the false data of such a statement as "He is a great motivator" or "She can really motivate her group." Not so! The people in the first example and the people in the second example are both totally responsible for their choice of behavior, just like you and me—and everyone else.

If the preceding paragraph is accurate—and it is!—then why are some teachers successful in (what appears to be) motivation, while others seem to always be lacking in this important talent? If we back up a bit, some fundamental understanding might help make this very clear. Motivation is a derivative of the Latin word *motere* which means "to move, to create action." Obviously, we have carried this into our language with *motor, motion, motivation.* If we want there to be motivation, there must be action, there must be movement. In fact, under close examination you will probably discover most motivation comes *after* the action. The feeling of accomplishment, the desire to go on, the commitment to achievement, usually is a result of some action. Without the initial movement, there will be little, if any, motivation. As music educators, we can quickly describe these great teachers we have seen "in action," and find they almost serve as a catalyst in causing others to "take action." The motivation (movement) is now in full swing. (It's analogous to priming the pump!)

The only absolute certainty of any motivation in our group is to put the responsibility on the one person whom we can control—ourself! That is a huge responsibility we often overlook in our daily teaching techniques. The skeptics can argue all they want, but history clearly shows it is always the leader, or teacher, who is responsible for the level of success of the group; herein lies the real key to successful motivation.

This could be a dismal article if we stopped here, but there is much to share with our students about this discovery. When students chide, "You don't motivate us!" you can congratulate them on their insight and explain their own success in life will not be determined by you and some false form of motivation (manipulation), but they must be directly responsible for their attitude, discipline, and motivation just as you are for yours! Now that's an educational breakthrough which can benefit each and every part of their lives!

Although I have never much enjoyed negative people, an individual's attitude, or mind-set, is certainly a personal choice, but when one chooses to be an educator and carries this negative attitude into the classroom, or (worse yet) a rehearsal, it then serves as "the standard" for the students—and, rest assured, they *will learn* to adapt it to their own behavior. Once again, the mirror is squarely reminding us of our need to create action, be positive, set high standards, and on and on. It is not going to happen until we motivate ourselves!

This reality is beautifully described in this magnificent quote by Haim Ginott:

> I have come to a frightening conclusion that I
> am the decisive element in the classroom. It's
> my personal approach that creates the climate.

It's my daily mood that makes the weather. As a teacher, I possess a tremendous power to make a tool of torture or an instrument of inspiration. I can humiliate or humor, hurt or heal. In all situations, it is my response that decides whether a crisis will be escalated or de-escalated and a child humanized or dehumanized.

Great isn't it?! Wisdom is always so simple, so direct, so honest! You might want to share this with some of your colleagues—and you know "just the one" who needs to read it, too!

Plato once said, "We will be braver and better if we engage and inquire than if we indulge in the idle fancy that we already know—or that it is of no use seeking to know what we do not know." As educators, it is our "mission" to seek out new knowledge, strive to grow personally, and set the example for those who will follow in our footsteps. The education process begins with us!

Keep smilin'!

*"Oversleeping will never
make dreams come true."*

# To Discipline
# or Not to Discipline?
# That Is the Question

Certainly we all want to be successful. *Success* is one
of those elusive terms which means different things to different
people. For some, it is a happy family, or a satisfying job,
maybe a cottage at the lake, a positive working atmosphere,
a strong financial base, plus many other ideas. But, most
certainly, the ability to make a choice keeps the human element
running at top speed to be successful at whatever the choice
is. What does it take to achieve, to realize, this success? We
have all heard the various clues which have been passed down
from our teachers and parents: the golden rule, a solid work
ethic, balanced living, a penny saved is a penny earned, don't
burn any bridges, persistence alone is omnipotent, treat every
day as though it is your last, the more education-the less
frustration, an apple a day and all that jazz. If it all had to be
condensed into one absolute quality, I think (note this is a
personal opinion!) it would be *discipline*. None of the above
can exist without discipline, and when you review your own

list of successful people, do they not all possess a strong sense of discipline? In our profession of music, discipline is a must—the discipline required to practice, attend rehearsals, spend extra time and effort outside of class, to fund-raise, to give up some of the "fun times" which are available to others. As educators, you have disciplined yourself to go to college, to study, to take exams, and now, to complete budget requests, year-long calendars, the discipline of disciplining, and just about everything else which comes into your day. The people who make it to the top seem to have this art of discipline down pat. Their self-discipline is constantly being refined. They have learned (through discipline) to make the most out of each and every moment, and they realize life is about "growing," and all growing requires discipline.

One of the first things I do in workshops is ask what the participants wish to gain from their efforts. The common answers are "Develop a better sense of motivation." "Gain a more positive attitude." "Learn to communicate more effectively." "Try to live up to my potential." "Feel good about myself." "Discover ways I can help others." All of these could be—*can* be—accomplished with a strong sense of discipline. There are volumes written about each and every subject mentioned; do these people have the discipline to sit down and read them? Do they discipline their time, their energies, their focus, their choices?

One particularly frustrated student found me after a recent seminar and said, "I agree with everything you said, but I'm not disciplined enough to discipline myself!" Well, that is a predicament of puzzling magnitude. We all have to come to grips with the fact that it is virtually up to us. Learning self-discipline is a habit just like any other behavioral habit. You don't just "get it" one day; it is a process of guiding one's efforts day in and day out. Even this takes a special kind of discipline.

When we all look back to our best teachers, leaders, and mentors, weren't they all people who created a great environment of discipline? Didn't they demand that you create a higher sense of discipline to accommodate their requests? Review your most successful times in life; weren't they coupled with high sense of discipline?

Too often the word *discipline* is associated with punishment, harshness, abuse, restriction, and the like. This is certainly not true. As teachers and leaders, we can approach the whole subject of discipline in a very positive and exciting way, revealing a realm of understanding which offers a host of benefits to the student and a key to all of the reasons for success mentioned in the first paragraph.

Since it is a learned behavior, it can be taught, nurtured, embellished, focused, and even planted or replanted in any person. In fact, the basis for everything presented in the motivational and leadership workshops is generated from discipline. Once this concept is understood and put into practice, everything from that point forth is quite easy. The minute anyone slips, the immediate question is, What is going on with your self-discipline? This, inevitably, will bring the individual back on track. Or, if it doesn't, then the individual has to take the responsibility for being undisciplined, which means that person will be exempt from enjoying any of the for-the-disciplined rewards. Strangely enough, there doesn't seem to be any age limit where this is beyond a person's understanding. In fact, younger students seem to grasp the concept very quickly and immediately begin to collect on the payoffs from their positive efforts, while the older skeptics often are very undisciplined about their discipline and, as a result, have a slower success rate. (Once again, the point is proven in this case!)

Rationalization is the arch enemy of discipline and it, too, is a learned habit. Some people are masters of rationalization, which makes them minors in discipline. Which are you? Which do you want your students to be?

Self-discipline is needed to achieve group discipline. Since music performance usually involves a group effort, the conclusion should be obvious:

## Successful groups are based on a strong foundation of discipline.

P.S. Avoid the temptation to "rationalize" the information in this article so you don't have to face the task of greater discipline!

> *"If we work upon marble, it will perish;*
> *if we work upon brass, time will efface it...but*
> *if we work upon immortal minds, we engrave*
> *on those tablets something which*
> *will brighten all eternity."*
> —Daniel Webster

# Daring to Look at the Whole Responsibility

As musicians, our vernacular centers around words and phrases like: *ensemble, blend, focus, unity, working together, responsibility, commitment, expression creating a unified mood, bringing a sense of "oneness" to the group, esprit de corps,* and so on. All of these thoughts are generated from the fundamental philosophy that there is more benefit for the individual via emphasis on *we* and *us* rather than *I* and *me.* Certainly, we all would agree we do give up a good measure of individuality when we become a part of a musical ensemble. We adjust everything from musical tastes to living schedules in order to accommodate the whole, the performance, the end result. The finest groups we know are those who set aside some of their individual, wide array of differences into one, common effort. The results create peak performances for both the listener as well as the performer. Ultimately, everyone grows because of the adjustment necessary in this group-goal endeavor.

This concept is nothing new; in fact, it is apparent in the

classic poem "The Law of the Jungle." For those who have never read this enlightening piece of writing—enjoy!

## The Law of the Jungle

Now here is the law of the jungle,
And it's as true and blue as the sky,
And those who obey it shall prosper,
But those who deny it shall die.
As the serpent who slithers the tree trunk,
The law runneth forward and back:
The strength of the pack is each wolf,
But the strength of each wolf is the pack!

Simple direct insightful. We would all agree, too! Although the radicals would scream it's communistic, the artist-musician would claim it *is* the only way to reach new levels of creating via any group. It is the essence of the meaning of ensemble—striving for new heights of unity, togetherness, oneness, center.

It would be easy to simply add a conclusive paragraph and claim another successful observation which brings new understanding to some, reinforcement for others, and is nonthreatening to most. However, that would be too easy and would not provoke much thought. It, quite simply, is too safe. There is more to this which will serve as a challenge for all of us. Let's pursue this next level of thinking.

If this philosophy (we/us) is the foundation of musical excellence, should we not bring that same kind of thinking into our approach to everything which directly or indirectly supports the musician, the rehearsals, the performance, etc.? Is it wise to have musical expectations, disciplines, even demands which are not congruent with our behavioral styles? The answers to these questions seem so elementary they do not deserve attention; yet, it always amazes me that a conductor or a teacher or a performer will convey one message, with instrument in hand, asking for our trust in accomplishing this wish, then in turn display a complete reversal of attitude following the rehearsal, performance, etc. The "survival reaction" is "Play safe. Don't trust this individual. Put up your defensive barriers, avoid confrontation. Be careful when dealing with this individual. The logic goes one step further: They are selfish, egotistical, manipulative, uncaring, self-centered, and so forth. The results are an immediate shift to the I/me concept ("What's in it for me?") which is counterproductive to the initial purpose. One step forward and three back!

Do we not have a responsibility, a duty, to bring those required musical attitudes and attributes into our persona? (How can we expect a "phrase of gentle serenity" when we have verbally "stabbed in the back" prior to the rehearsal?) If there is to be beauty in music, it has to come from the performer(s), and if there is no beauty in the performer, then, the product becomes an act, a pretense—a lie! This Dr. Jekyll/ Mr. Hyde communication becomes a great (if not the greatest) barrier in achieving a peak performance in music—not to mention everything else in life.

Defensive actions, negative attitudes, fear of risk, avoidance of change, and stringent protective behavior all stem from insecurity and fear. They are positions our personalities assume to protect the individual. They create walls and obstacles which prevent communication, and cooperation, and they strongly reinforce the I/me pattern of living, which is counterproductive to the community ("with unity") environment desired for an artistic experience.

The point is, as teachers, performers, conductors, and students, we must constantly discipline our own behavior or action so it aligns our being with our desires. Consider having a Weight Watchers meeting at the local Baskin Robbins ice cream parlor. That would be ridiculous! Is it not just as paradoxical to assume total cooperation in the rehearsal hall and yet be unwilling to cooperate with the administration when they make a decision which benefits the entire school, but infringes on our personal wishes? And the answer is: It depends on the situation! Allow me to suggest that we are not discussing individual instances, but rather viewing an overall question of attitude. How do you approach each one of these problems? Ask yourself, Do I want my students to mirror my attitude during rehearsal? Are my methods congruent with what I believe to be my mission in life? Am I asking of myself what I am asking of others? If the answer is yes, then the rewards you receive from everything you do will far exceed your expectations, which will offer you more fuel for future creations. If the answer is no, it would behoove you to reevaluate the why of all your choices. Herein lies a tremendous opportunity to bring a new sense of zest and joy into your life, as well as all those around you.

Gilbert Arland wrote, "When an archer misses the mark, he turns and looks for the fault within himself. Failure to hit the bull's-eye is never the fault of the target. To improve your aim, improve yourself." It is true that we cannot direct the wind, but we can adjust the sails.

We can have some say-so in the results because of our approach, our willingness to cooperate, and our belief that we do have value simply because of who we are. Since we are what we repeatedly do, excellence is not a part-time standard. It is not something we turn on and off; it is a habit, and it reveals itself in all other parts of our life. Our art (music/teaching) is nothing more than a manifestation of who we are. That, friend, is an incredible responsibility, particularly when that who-we-are will determine, through our students, who others will grow to be. This does not begin and end in the rehearsal room.

We all want the best for our groups and our students. We all desire to produce quality, or more altruistically, to make a positive difference in the world. Nobody ever attains eminent success by simply doing what is required. Success comes from the amount of "extra," which is over and above the required. Therein lies the formula for greatness and ultimate distinction. We must constantly demand of ourselves that we go beyond what we already know—to improve ourselves, to seek new growth for ourselves, to (if you will) embrace change instead of fear it, to continually open our ability to accept others and their insecurities, and to love even those people who seem to be in disagreement and thereby avoid the temptation to prolong the I/me game of life via some form of retaliation. The process one must go through to accomplish this is ongoing. Security is such a myth. Only those who admit their insecurities and shortcomings are truly secure!

Security is an attitude. The spirit, the desire for excellence, and the will to achieve quality are all attitudes which will endure. These are so much more important than the events which allow them to be!

We have much to do to bring about beauty, peace, joy, happiness, and expression of who we are. Let the music begin!

*"A mistake is at least evidence that
someone tried to do something."*

# The Proof Is
# in the Pudding

Education is full of little axioms which we all pass over somewhere in our educational classes in college and soon forget in the midst of the everyday tasks at hand, but they crop up several years later and make more sense now that we have the experiences to go with them. So much of what we teach in the leadership workshops is centered on the things we already know but fail to put into practice each day. If we are to succeed at anything when we are dealing with other people, we had better be in command of the laws of leadership. This short article dwells on one such law:

**I hear—I forget;**
**I see—I remember;**
**I do—I understand!**

I HEAR—I FORGET! It's true! We remember about ten percent of what we hear. In terms of teaching (leadership), we can quickly see the application of this to any facet of the musical scene. How many times have we spent countless hours going over the very same material? Lecturing until we were blue in the face, only to have a student continue to make the same mistake time and time again! If we are to follow this formula, we would have to say everything ten times to insure the student (follower) would completely understand. And then, of course, the next time we run into the same problem, we are up for another ten swings at the ball before there is any guarantee of hitting it.

Maybe there is a better way!

I SEE—I REMEMBER. Have you ever watched a group play a concert with their heads buried in the music? On the podium the conductor is frantically trying to get the attention of the group so she or he can institute some musical interpretation. All too common, isn't it? And we all know the wonderful feeling of looking out on a group and seeing several sets of eyes meet ours, ready to bring a new sense of emotion at the whim of the baton. It's great!

Retention rate when students are watching jumps to twenty-four percent. Simply by keeping the eyes on a teacher, the students will retain an additional fourteen percent. So, in any form of communication, it is a necessity to make eye contact with those around you. Never give instructions without making sure the students (followers) are watching you. Demand and command eye contact.

Maybe there is a better way!

I DO—I UNDERSTAND! Ah yes! When we participate in anything, our level of retention jumps to eighty percent. If you truly want those you are leading to grasp any concept, you must get them to do it! A more pragmatic way of saying this is quit talking so much, quit demonstrating so much—have the person do it more! Experience is always the best teacher in the world.

What does this have to do with leadership?

When we pass out the assignments for various leadership roles, the instructions often stop there. We assume the person is going to be able to deal with his or her peers. That is not always (in fact rarely!) the case. Thus, much time is wasted as these leaders go about telling their followers what to do, (ten percent retention), showing them what to do by doing it themselves as a demonstrator (twenty-four percent retention), and very little time on having the followers (learners) actually doing, (eighty percent retention). And, as we all know, the success of any leader is in direct proportion to their ability to produce excellence in the people they are leading.

I am reminded of an instance at a summer band camp when the section leader of the clarinets was having a sectional rehearsal. The problems were many and the poor leader was frustrated, exasperated, and ready to cash it all in. She kept taunting, "You aren't playing the right notes!" Then would follow a lecture about the importance of learning each note and during this one-way sharing of words, the various players would gaze around and check their watches. The next day she had advanced to walking down the line, planting herself stoically in front of each clarinetist and demanding they watch and listen as she ripped off an 8 measure passage which would make most symphony players stand up and take notice. Although it was impressive, when the section would then put their instruments to their mouths, little, if any, improvement could be detected. The frustration level grew in both leader and followers.

It is at this point many people throw in the towel, but this story has a happy ending. By day three, the apparent lack of improvement was evident to everyone. Our leader refocused the energy and began to have the various people in the section play for her. Note by note, person by person, measure by measure, they went. Pencils began to come out of cases and pockets, silent fingerings were being executed while others worked on certain notes, cooperation in the section was evident as information was passed from student to student. And the sound improved! And as the sound improved, the momentum grew, the excitement increased, which led to a better sound— and the circle of success was in action.

When the final concert was performed, the clarinet section displayed a degree of musicianship and technique far beyond what anybody had thought possible. The credit was given to their section leader. The great teachers are always the ones who can support us in going above and beyond our self-inflicted limits.

Now, if you want your leaders to benefit from this article, *don't* read it to them and *don't* put it on the board for them to read, but sit down with them and go over it together. Make a list of "to do's" which will improve the group, then have the group do them!

Let's not talk about creating excellence or observe those who have created excellence, but let's go about creating excellence. Real leadership always comes out of action. The proof is in the pudding! Take some action!

*"Trouble may ring your door bell, but
it's your fault if you invite it in."*

# The Essence of
# What Makes a
# Special Event Special

Special events always seem to bring out the best in our groups. The students' intentions are at a higher level and the aura of the performance atmosphere adds an extra boost of positive energy which focuses all the efforts on a common goal. Maybe that's why we call them special events.

We all know the value of goal-setting. In a very real sense, isn't that what a concert or performance is? The attainment of the goal is the reward for the young musician's investment over the weeks and months. With the popularity of festivals, band exchanges, trips to exotic and popular locations, many music students are exposed to an exciting array of special events. The educational value of such a project can be beyond measure, or it can be a rather ho-hum experience, depending on the habits which are developed via the day-to-day standards expected and achieved in the music curriculum. If we want to make an event really special, then that goal is based on making each rehearsal a special event.

We are a society of instant gratification. Our lives are built around a microwave approach to almost all facets of living. It's a buy-now-pay-later theme which serves as the basis for so many of the decisions we make. (Let me be quick to add this is not a positive or negative judgement call concerning this popular pattern. It is simply a fact of our present day lifestyle.) If caution is not taken, special events can become a case of the tail wagging the dog. For example, if students' participation in music is based on where the group is going on the spring trip, we have missed the point—drastically! In this case, the destination has become more important to the young traveler than the journey itself. If so, what are we teaching other than just another quick fix?

The master educator ensures that every day will be a special event by creating an environment where each student is special. From the warm-up exercises to the final rehearsal notes, the challenge is to have every musician walk out of the class feeling as though he or she has added to his or her growing vocabulary of musical expression and understanding. If that primary goal is overshadowed or takes a back seat to the upcoming trip to Happyland, U.S.A., then what is the point of calling it music education? We might as well set up a class in "Effective Trip-Taking."

Many concerned music educators have avoided participating in all kinds of out-of-school trips, and festivals, based on the fear that the event might produce a negative impact on the whole of the musical program. This is certainly one form of protecting the musical integrity of the curriculum. At the same time, it might be seen as a deprivation of other linked educational opportunities. Perhaps the argument, or discussion, is not about the worth of special events, but rather how the students are prepared to gain the most positive growth and development from the experience. Once again, we find that responsibility lies directly on the shoulders of the director and the pre-event planning and teaching which determines the value for each participant.

There is much to be gained in terms of self-discipline, character development, group cooperation, appropriate behavior patterns, acknowledgment opportunities, high-level responsibility, dedication, commitment, and building the organization's sense of worth as a part of the special event's offerings. However, the special event only offers a stage for this endeavor; it does not guarantee that these important self-improvement goals will be attained. Rest assured, whatever behavior is expected and accepted during daily rehearsals will be vividly recreated from the moment the group leaves until the schedule is completed. If they are well-disciplined and focused during practices, then they will demonstrate this learning and make you, the director, very proud outside the school surroundings—and deservedly so. On the other hand, if the group has trouble staying on task during each day's class and you find yourself in a constant state of frustration, you can expect an amplification of the same behavior during the special event. The group simply isn't mature enough to be exposed to a new environment; it is obvious they are not in control within the walls of the rehearsal room. Herein lies the opportunity to set up a curriculum which will give them the road map to personal responsibility and reward them with some rather exciting possibilities for the future—not to mention it will remove your frustration. Each rehearsal can become a microcosm of the special event. The lesson plans teaching the value of group responsibility are endless when the organization embraces this mutual goal.

Shouldn't the fundamental theme of our teaching be that music education *is* a special event?! One does not have to travel to Orlando, London, or even Happyland, U.S.A., to enjoy a special event. We can create it tomorrow in our rehearsal by sharing an artistic experience on the B-flat scale. If that is too simplistic or boring for the students, then we might want to review our own standards. The music itself must be the unifying factor. Then, and only then, are we ready to take the next step forward as we proudly share our musical talents and skills for others to enjoy. When the students, director, staff, administrators, and parents observe excellence in the performance level both on and off the stage, then we truly have created a special event.

# Part Two

## It's All in Your Attitude

# It's All in Your Attitude

$P$eople behave according to how they feel, not what they know. Therefore, attitude is the basis of everything we do. Our lifestyle becomes a manifestation of our attitude.

"Attitude" is such a nebulous word, isn't it? It has been abused, overused, misused, and certainly confused. What does it really mean?

*Attitude*: a mental position with regard to a fact or a state. A feeling or emotion toward a fact or a state. The position of someone in relation to a frame of reference.

As each hour goes by we learn more and more, and gain the ability to program ourselves and have our circumstances (environment) reflect that very thinking. It really is such a simple choice: Do I want to feel good or bad, happy or sad, excited or depressed, etc. We, all of us, have total control of our thoughts, our attitudes, and when we understand how they guide our daily behavior, we then see the high priority they should have within our lives.

"Happy people live in happy worlds, and sad people live in sad worlds...and it is all the same world." It is truly a matter of attitude!

The following section of the book will give you some pragmatic hints about the development of this key factor. It is such an exciting study and we are only seeing the tip of the iceberg at this point. When people talk about the twenty-first century, there is a common agreement among them that the major focus will be on human potential, or developing a positive, productive attitude.

There is great information in this section that you can put to work immediately!

*"You can't do everything, but
you can do something."*

# Getting Serious
# about Being Positive

The title of this article should provoke some questions in your mind. Isn't *positive* generally related with "happy," "upbeat," "fun," or "not negative"? Although this is the popular premise, it is an incorrect interpretation and one which can keep many from further exploring the unlimited potential of the student. Many educational researchers have confirmed that a positive environment is the most conducive for maximum learning results. Immediately our minds conjure up these visions of classes filled with frivolity and unrealistic happiness in a contrived situation overflowing with artificial sunshine, which we are certain is reserved for the carefully chosen study group and definitely is impossible in the realm of everyday teaching. Therefore, we dismiss the possibility of what a positive approach could mean to our students, our program, and ourselves and carelessly conclude it is impractical, idealistic, and has no application in the real world of music education. Yet, when we study the outstanding programs across the nation, there is one common theme: Everything is based on a positive foundation.

We have all heard the story of the young man who was diligently practicing his clarinet for the upcoming auditions. After several unsuccessful attempts to master his etude, he threw his instrument down and announced in disgust, "I'm going to really mess up on this playing test tomorrow!" Jumping to his feet, his eager father reprimanded, "You must be positive!" And the aspiring young musician retorted, "You're right! I'm *positive* I'm going to really mess up on this playing test tomorrow!"

In this case, the young man was really dealing with the essence of what *positive* is all about. On the other hand, his father was offering a weak (at best) solution to his son's predicament; just "thinking" it is going to get better is self-deception at the highest level. (Remember the "think technique" from the Meredith Wilson's *Music Man?*)

Our friend Webster defines *positive* as "constituting a motion which is definite, unyielding, certain in its pattern; not fictitious, real, logically affirmative."

Doesn't this also describe the attributes of a master teacher? Think about your most effective and influential mentors; didn't they bring these same positive traits to the learning process? Now let's go one step further and analyze our own teaching efforts.

DO WE CONSTITUTE A DEFINITE FORWARD MOTION? Let's not confuse filling up time with information as a definite forward motion. Although spontaneity is always a signature of a fine teacher, it must be above and beyond the careful planning of each day's goals.

ARE WE UNYIELDING AND CERTAIN IN OUR PAT-TERNS? When we settle for less-than-excellence, that's exactly what we get. It is important that our students understand our level of expectation. In truth, they do. Simply follow them from one class to the next and observe their behavior change according to the expectations of the teacher.

ARE WE NON-FICTITIOUS, REAL, AND LOGICALLY AFFIRMATIVE? We have all fallen into the trap of being unrealistic—much like the middle school band director who insists on playing a grade VI piece of music, or the private teacher who demands three hours of practice each day, or else! (Though we have fulfilled the non-yielding aspect of our positive definition, we have violated the "real" issue.) And, when we address the area of the logically affirmative, we find this is the pivotal point of judgement which separates the good teachers from the positively great ones.

It is pointless (many think detrimental) to affirm anyone who has not accomplished the given task or assignment. That certainly doesn't mean we stop encouraging, inspiring, or supporting them, but we must be honest. Learn the fine art of correcting a person's efforts without damaging their self-image. To keep from hurting a student's feelings, we are often tempted to lower the standards so they will feel the accomplishment of the goal and, as a result, raise their self-esteem. (It also means we do not have to confront the situation and the aftermath of emotion which comes with personal disappointment, so the path of least resistance seems to be an inviting option.) Unfortunately, the short-lived pseudo-satisfaction is quickly replaced by the understanding that we shifted the rules in the middle of the game. Lowering expectations often backfires and leaves the student with a sense of false security about the integrity of the original goals. (Remember when you were very young and played checkers with an adult who let you win? There was an empty feeling of self-doubt, wasn't there?) Conversely, when we fall short but are met with the "affirmative logic" to immediately go back to the drawing board, hone our techniques and skills, and reach deeper into our creative potential, then the disappointment of not achieving the desired goal is replaced with the drive to try it again, knowing there will be a higher level of self-improvement which will honestly and positively raise one's self-esteem. Now that is positive teaching.

As we begin this new school year, we have new students, a new mix of personalities within our groups, and an opportunity to put some fresh new thoughts and ideas into practice. There is no second chance at a first impression. What better time to get serious about being positive?!

*"Where I was is destroyed, where I
am stands condemned, where I shall
be is just now being built."*

# Achieving Success

When we all have the potential to succeed at almost anything we choose, why do so few people attain a high level performance? What do the top achievers know that others do not? What habits do the successful individuals bring to their life patterns which ensures their attainment of personal and professional goals?

It has been said we use only six percent of our mind power, and the latest research is now saying it may only be two percent for normal daily behavior. We are like powerful computers with no instruction manual for success. The great minds of past and present may not have been as great as we all thought, but merely were men and women wise enough to delve into their untapped potential and uncover a limitless supply of possibilities. What was it they discovered? What is the key that unlocks our otherwise dormant abilities? How do we master this technique?

The concept of self-fulfilling prophecy is one which every one of us must deal with in our quest for excellence. In truth, we get what we expect. We never do better than we think we can. We live into the pictures and visions we place in our minds; thus the familiar phrase, "Whether we think we can or whether we think we can't, we're always right."

There have been countless Pygmalion experiments over the years all yielding the same results: If we can change the self-concept of the individual, the behavior results will match. We become who we think we are.

The implications of this understanding in the world of education are far-reaching. If we know, for the most part, students will not perform beyond our expectation level, then we also know the same is true of us. Are we constantly learning and grooming ourselves to be the best we can be, or have we opted to fall into the comfortable trap of, "it's good enough?"

Do we see ourselves as producing a quality environment where we can constantly improve the understanding and performance of our students, or are we simply glad just to get through the day, week, month, and year? In short, do we hold high expectations for ourselves knowing it will determine the success of our classes? These can be very uncomfortable questions, for they confront the very foundation of our value as meaningful teachers who effectively bring new insights to our students so they will live more prosperous lives. At the same time, they offer us an opportunity to take an inventory of our present situation and either move forward or make necessary adjustments according to the findings.

Success is not an accident. It is a predictable pattern and, like any good tested formula, it works when the individual works. In many cases, the price of success is doing what others don't want to do, or going the extra mile when others have chosen to give up.

If it is so easy, why don't more people participate? Why do most people live far below their potential? The number one reason: the inability to delay gratification.

Many are tempted to choose fun and easy over difficult and necessary, or tension-relieving over goal-achieving. We know that bad habits are easy to form, but hard to live with, while good habits are hard to form, but easy to live with. The obvious choice is to create positive habits which avoid the quick fix and offer long-range benefits. Every self-improvement program, from weight watchers to time management, is useless without this fundamental ingredient: the personal belief and self-discipline needed to delay gratification until the envisioned goal is attained. Once this is in place, the journey begins. Even after arrival, the next step is a wise maintenance program that continues the process in the future.

Where does one start? What is the first step? Is this just more mumbo-jumbo or can it really work for me?

Different programs work for different people. However, every success story has one common theme: the commitment of the individual to see it through to the end. A half-hearted effort produces half-hearted results.

The following guidelines serve as a launch pad:

**1. SET CLEARLY DEFINED GOALS.** There is little or no personal motivation without goals. The more detailed and defined the goals, the more energy you will produce to reach them. So often goals are too general, i.e., "I want to be happy." "I want to be successful." "My goal is to have people respect me."

These are admirable, but goal-setting needs to be specific. Use calendar dates as goal markers. Create personal deadlines. Make certain the goals are measurable and attainable and be certain to write them down. They serve as your road map to success. Perhaps one of your goals would be to learn how to set goals. It is a very exciting process, but takes delayed gratification to accomplish the task.

**2. COMMIT TO YOUR AREA OF EXCELLENCE.** Unless we commit to excellence, we are doomed to mediocrity. Throw yourself into the pursuit of excellence. Spend time studying and learning everything you can about your chosen area of expertise. Beware of complacency. Surround yourself with others who have a like interest and passion and support this mutual interest. Rekindle the childhood enthusiasm which offers direction to inquisition. Become an expert in some facet of life and invite those around you to participate and enjoy the benefits of learning and growing towards a higher level of competence.

**3. REVIEW YOUR GOALS AND MEASURE YOUR DAILY PROGRESS.** Out of sight, out of mind. Remember that the mind leads us in the direction of its most dominant thought. The positive effects of "self-talk" are well-known to those who practice the art of visioning. See yourself achieving the intended short-range and long-range goals. Keep your success-pictures at the forefront of your conscious mind. Much unhappiness comes from not knowing one's destination; therefore, constantly remind yourself of how far you've come and where you need to still go. Build on what you know. Success builds success. Be faithful to your Master Plan. Treat it as you would the most important thesis assignment of your career: it could well be.

**4. STAY ON TASK: PERSISTENCE IS SELF-DISCIPLINE IN ACTION.** If you want to increase your success rate, increase your failure rate. There will be adversity; accept it, even embrace it. Every time you meet a situation which slows down your progress, ask yourself, "What is there for me to learn?" Within the problem is certain to be the clue for the next forward move.

Unfortunately, it is popular to quit after so many false starts or thwarted efforts. In the classic words of a world leader who repeated a grade in school, Winston Churchill, "Never give up. Never, never give up." Where would the world be today if Sir Winston would have chosen to quit after his educational setback? Every breakthrough in our modern world is a result of some persistent (often stubborn) person who refused to accept defeat. There is no substitute for fulfilled commitment. It is the primary fuel for a healthy self-esteem.

**5. ACCEPT TOTAL RESPONSIBILITY.** See yourself as the cause and not the effect. This simple premise offers a very strong personal power base for personal motivation. When something goes awry, accept the responsibility and avoid the temptation to blame someone. Blame gets us "off the hook," but it also violates our responsibility factor. Focus on solutions, not problems. Count on yourself to come through in every situation. Pay the price and pay it in advance. This is where delayed gratification is put to the test. The more responsible we are, the better we like ourselves.

**6. ACKNOWLEDGE YOUR SUPPORTING CAST.** Dynamic people have the ability to uplift the spirits of those around them. Your personal health is in direct proportion to your ability to get along with others. Let other people know and understand your goals so they can support you in the effort. You can't go at it alone. Eventually you are going to need some one's help, expertise, direction, or whatever. Everyone likes to be around a successful person, so share the glory of the victory with all those who played a role in your accomplishment. You will quickly discover an eager group of people awaiting the opportunity to work with you in the future.

A person with clear, focused goals will outstrip a genius every time. Success awaits us all. Will we take the road less traveled? The game of self-discipline takes life-long study, practice, and discipline. It may not be the "will to succeed" that counts as much as the "will to prepare to succeed." The above six-step formula is a preparation course aimed at achieving success. Once we have reached the summit of this mountain (goal), we quickly see other mountains (goals) which require further self-discipline.

A more simplistic approach came from a friend who has enjoyed success throughout his life. I asked him one day, "To what do you attribute all your many accomplishments in life?" He smiled and said quietly, "I found out what unsuccessful people do and I don't do it."

Enough said.

*"Failure is the line of least persistence."*

# It's All in Your Attitude...and Theirs (Creating Winners!)

Another school year is initiated and every band, choir, and orchestra director has carefully marked the calendar with the various performances for the upcoming academic year. Every attempt to avoid conflicts with track meets, SAT testing, student government conventions, and spring proms has been made. "Let the games begin...!"

As we begin, let us take a moment to highlight some of the basic principles we can share with the students through our musical talents. Although we are interested in correct notes, accurate counting, phrasing, dynamics, etc., we also must focus on our responsibility to share fundamental guidelines to living which can adapt to each and every part of life. Herein lies the "secret" of the Master Teacher who makes a positive difference in the life of each student.

Let's focus this article on the concepts of winning. Competition is such an integral part of our society, and we have seen it grow in our musical activities with the increase of local and national festivals across the country. Although many people have very strong opinions for and against the value of competition, it is deeply rooted within our educational system, from report cards to making the varsity athletic team. We have auditions for chair placement, who sings the solo, organizational officers, awards at the annual banquet, and so forth. In this "living lab," we have a perfect opportunity to develop a healthy and productive attitude toward winning, and also define (through role modeling) the behavior of a winner.

This is easily accomplished by comparing the actions of a winner and a loser. Of course, what we must keep in mind is winning and losing are merely labels to identify the way we handle various situations. Let's be clear that winning and first place are not necessarily synonymous. Likewise, losing and last place do not mean the same thing. With the emphasis in our society on Number One, it is easy for students (as well as adults) to conclude, "Unless we are first place, we are losers!" This logic leads to the accompanying behavior of a loser. And we all know the loser's attitude is one of much frustration and low productivity. This ultimately leads to giving up, quitting. At this point, we have little chance of "educating" if the child is no longer in the class.

With this in mind, here are some "trademarks" of winners and losers, and ideas we can share with our students to insure they always win in every endeavor.

DEALING WITH MISTAKES. Mistakes are a part of life. Each day is a series of trials and errors, and the successful people are the ones who can make the best of each and every situation. Losers are interested in "justifying" an error. They will explain and explain why something doesn't work. They can communicate in detailed terms what went wrong and how it went wrong, and why they weren't at fault. Winners will take the mistake as a sign to correct and will immediately go about making the necessary adjustments. They are solution-oriented and realize the value of moving quickly to avoid holding up the entire operation. (Identifying a flat tire and the cause of the mishap rarely gets the car back on the road. Change the tire!)

SETTING A GOAL FOR EVERY ACTIVITY. An individual with a winning attitude will achieve excellence regardless of the price they have to pay or regardless of how trivial the task.

They are incredibly persistent, self-motivated, and do not accept the standards of others, but set their own standards. They always produce—always! Losers seem to fall short of every goal they set. When this happens, they tend to bolster their own sagging self-image by blaming other people and circumstances for their shortcomings. They always know why everything doesn't work, but rarely have little to contribute to solve the problem at hand.

Music is such a great avenue for short- and long-term goal setting. There are so many opportunities to produce and recognize excellence, from beginning scales to concertos.

UNDERSTAND "GIVE AND TAKE." A true winner knows real victory comes from giving to other people. They see that the value in learning, acquiring, developing, and growing is to share it with others. They think in terms of we and us rather than the I and me. Their behavior is always caring, open, and non-selfish. Losers are always skeptical and suspicious. They feel if anyone finds out what they know, it could be used against them, therefore they spend much of their energy closing off, hiding, and creating barriers so others will be confused.

So much of music education can demonstrate the benefits of giving: e.g., performance, rehearsals, extra effort, teaching others, sharing parts. It is simply making the behavior of a winner a habit.

VALUE OF COMPETITION. A winner realizes the benefits of competition are not in the final comparisons, but in the self-growth gained in the preparation and the competition experience. They see competition as a game and not as an all-or-nothing determination of any kind of self-worth. They play the game at a 110-percent energy level and find great personal satisfaction in playing as opposed to making the value of the game the results (score). Losers will pretend they really don't want to win, therefore if they lose, they have a perfect excuse: "I didn't really care in the first place. If I really cared, I could have won."

Music presents so many opportunities we can use to support personal growth. Each day offers a chance to better our discipline, from sitting straight in the chair to recognizing every key change. Every rehearsal and performance can represent a victory if we recognize it—more winning habits.)

THE GIFT OF CHOICE. Each moment of each day, we have to make choices. Choosing to be in music is such an important choice. These are the students who go the extra mile. Winners understand they have to be responsible for choosing how to invest their time, spend their energy, and determine their attitude. They operate knowing there is no *need* to be in a musical organization and it is a privilege to have the *choice* to join. They honor and respect their choice. Losers tend to feel as though they are trapped in the group, and that the group should be dedicated to making them happy. Of course, they continue to display a weak attitude so the group is forced to give them attention.

Music can represent a perfect situation for acknowledgment of positive contribution. It can be an arena for finding the good in each and every participant. We can make it very fashionable to be a winner.

Of course, these attributes can apply to each and every part of life. As music teachers, we have such a prime opportunity to develop these qualities through every teaching experience. We can make a difference when this becomes the philosophical foundation of our life contribution—sometimes called a *job*, but so much more than that.

It would be wonderful if each student went on to play and sing throughout their life, but we all know how the instruments and choir robes find their way to the attic. However, each student will go on to become a working member of society. Knowing this, it seems crucial we continue to bring out the best in all of them and give them the guidelines to success which will apply to anything they choose in life.

Let's dedicate our energies to creating winners. Here's to a great year of many victories!

*"Courage is not the absence of fear;
it is the conquest of it."*

# Dealing with Feelings of Insecurity

One of the real advantages that band people have in life centers around the discipline we all learn in our band programs. Besides staying in line and learning our parts, there is also the most important discipline of dealing with other people. We have to work together or there is no forward motion in the band. Whether we happen to like this or that person is of no consequence, we must get along, or the band suffers (which, ultimately, means we lose!).

When there is any conflict between or among people, it generally stems from a kind of behavior that "turns off" someone else. (Adults label it a personality conflict, which is simply a fancy title describing a situation where two or more people don't agree.) Often the term *insecure* is used as the reasoning for certain behavioral patterns. "He acts like that because he is insecure." "She talks about other people because she is insecure about herself." "John isn't going to try out for drum major because he feels very insecure about his chances."

The truth is we are all insecure. None of us are experts on everything, and each day of our lives we are faced with problems where we have to risk to solve them so we can move on. (Of course when we risk, we also set ourselves up for failure—and many people simply cannot face failure.) Therefore, if we can understand our own insecurities and how we treat them, it will allow us to see why other people behave as they do, and through this understanding, we can effectively eliminate most (if not all) personality conflicts and create stronger bands through our personal leadership and role-modeling. Who wouldn't want that? Let's see how people deal with these common feelings and how we can learn to use them to our advantage.

There are six basic reactions to feelings of insecurity. As they are described, you will probably be able to recognize someone in your band who fits this category. The important thing is we learn to positively use the information to help the person grow. (This article will be a real beneficial challenge for the leaders in the band.)

WITHDRAWAL. Individuals who react to insecurity through withdrawal simply hide within a shell of silence. They will never volunteer to step forward on any project. They are living in constant fear of being picked out of the crowd. (The thought of embarrassment is unbearable.)

To communicate effectively with these individuals, be very gentle in your approach. Harshness and criticism will drive them further back into their shells to the point they may eventually quit rather that face the fear of failing.

AGGRESSIVE SARCASM. We all recognize the person who always has to make a comment and put others down. The only way the individual can make themselves look good is by making others look bad.

The most productive way to deal with this kind of insecurity is to communicate with this person on a one-to-one basis. Never deal with the aggressiveness in front of the group. It only reinforces this behavior as an attention-getter and does nothing to curb the insecurity.

SILLINESS. Do you have the band clown in your group? This person has to make a joke about everything and is always good for a laugh, even in the most serious moments.

A "true friend" will address the clown and let him or her

know the humor is appreciated, but is not necessary to insure the person's worth to the band. In other words, there is a time and place for everything. (Remember, some people laugh to keep from crying or act silly in order to avoid painful seriousness.)

INDIFFERENCE. These people are the few who never seem to care about anything. They don't have moments of joy or sadness—they just go through the motions, never demonstrating any readable emotions.

These are very difficult individuals to get to because there appears to be nothing to discuss. If music is a form of expression, then the necessity to express is fundamental, so the emotions have to come to the surface. Often this reaction of indifference is a result of being hurt in a past experience, so these people feel if they don't care then they won't be hurt. Unfortunately this behavior is self-destructing and is keeping the individual from enjoying the basic reason for being in the band in the first place. Patience is primary in handling this individual. Take your time. Progress is slow.

CONFORMITY. Here we have the persons who stay in the middle of the road on everything. If everyone else votes yes, they will vote yes also—even if they disagree with the concept. These people focus all their energy on not being different. They feel as long as they are in the middle of the pack, nobody will pick them out, and they won't have to confront their insecurity.

We must remind these people that they are easy prey for everyone. (As long as we have huge numbers in this category, fads will reign supreme, and everyone will devote their efforts to being just like everyone else, instead of themselves.) Usually you can reason with these people; unfortunately, their understanding may be just another form of conformity. Lots of time and energy is necessary here!

COMPENSATION. Here is the person who recognizes the insecurity and decided to do something about it, rather than choose one of the other five non-productive options. These people have the same fears, the same considerations, the same feelings of failure, the same desires to quit that anyone else may have. The difference is they don't quit. Instead they risk, knowing that every success usually has six to eight failures as a prior investment.

How many times have you heard the clever little sayings such as "No pain, no gain" or "When the going gets tough, the tough get going." The truth is these all describe the compensator, the individual who realizes a weakness and goes about solving it through study, practice, extra hours, volunteer duty, courtesy, and lots of blood, sweat, and tears.

A very wise young lady put it quite simply in one of my workshops. She said, "The only difference between a successful person and one who is not is the successful person decides to go for it in spite of their fears." Profound!

As you head into tomorrow, how are you going to deal with your sense of insecurity? Perhaps the most helpful thing we can all do is join together in helping one another conquer our fears and support those around us in taking the risk, but being the first ones on hand to help them if they fail.

We quickly see insecurity is a given in this thing called growing. The choice of how we deal with it is the key to our success. The choice seems obvious: Let's band together!

*"Things may come to those who wait, but only the things left by those who hustle."*
— Abraham Lincoln

# Argue for Your Limitations and You Get To Own Them

Part of the music education profession seems to focus on the development of a personal "laundry list" of recognized (and verified) reasons to justify the progress (or lack of it) of the music program. The typical conversation that is standard patter at any gathering of music instructors seems to be a verbal trade-off of the worst problems with each person's home teaching situation. It's the old "well I can top that one" syndrome—the proverbial "fish story" in reverse. For those of you who graduated from college and did not develop your own list (if that is possible), here are some suggestions that have "stood the test of time" and are acceptable in most situations where your accountability might be questioned.

MY MUSIC PROGRAM ISN'T BETTER BECAUSE:
   A. We're forced to work in inadequate facilities. (Check plans for future building before you use this one.)
   B. Lack of sufficient budget. (This is always good! Caution: Look at the last five years' inventory before making any accusations.)

C. My administration doesn't understand the value of the arts. (Better look into the administrator's area of degree study prior to tossing this one out—it could be embarrassing.)

D. We lack a supportive booster organization. (Be certain your first trumpet player isn't the son of the booster president before using this one.)

E. Our school has too much emphasis on athletics and none on music. (This is a common one—coaches often become principals. You might be digging your own grave.)

F. The students aren't motivated and they all have a terrible attitude. (TILT! Avoid this common reason or a second-year psychology student will have a field day with your ego!)

G. We don't have enough time in the school curriculum for music. (There's potential here, but carefully research your neighboring music teacher's schedule—the facts might be used to void your argument.)

H. This community is culturally deprived and doesn't understand anything about quality music. (This may be true,. but to antagonize or ridicule is a guaranteed way to lose the crucial support that you need—bite your tongue in this case.)

I. All of our equipment is outdated junk. (Another valid point but make sure you: 1. Have personnel to play the requested new equipment, and 2. Have a plan on how you can help get new instruments. Administrators are really touchy about "all take, no give" situations.)

J. The elementary and junior high teachers aren't doing their job preparing the upcoming musicians. ("Sticks and stones may break my bones, but words will never hurt me." Cooperation is needed. To add unrest to an already weak situation will undoubtedly reflect on you.)

K. There is no support staff to aid in the already overloaded schedule. (Again, have your plan for the future at hand—without it you give yourself away as a victim of circumstance. Also, you run the danger of showing off your management skills, or lack of them.)

L. The school faculty is jealous. (Hint: Poking a stick in a hornet's nest will insure the "sting"—no pun intended.)

M. My salary doesn't support my living standard so I have to take time away from my work to subsidize my income. I need to make more money. (Yes, and so does every other teacher in your school. Let's suppose you did succeed in getting a substantial increase. Are you ready to deal with the problem when your fellow teachers discover the situation? It is a valid argument for all of education.)

N. My spouse doesn't understand the demands on my time. (Any profession can be time-consuming. Don't blame failure of either professional or personal life on the other—it spotlights your inability to make mature choices.)

O. My music parents think they can run the program better than I can. (Can they? Do they know exactly where their energies will mean the most to their sons and daughters? Have they been part of the education? Is everyone working for the same goal? Does everyone see the big picture?)

P. There is too much emphasis on competition and not enough on education. (Restated: There is too much emphasis on being number one. When anyone truly understands the price of having to always be in first place, they will quickly give it up: the end result is defeat. All the first place trophies in the world will never replace the joy of the personal growth to be had by simply "going for it." Winning is giving 100 percent!)

Q. I have an assistant director who would rather be the director. We don't work together well. (Go back and read "K" again! Before you "go for broke," be sure you have explored every avenue of resolution with the assistant. It's a rather obvious case of "united we stand, divided we fall." Does your assistant understand this concept?)

R. The school policies don't consider the band program. (Translated: The school policies do not consider my personal wants and needs. Usually, sound reasoning combined with a meaningful alternative can get most policies amended. Check the history of the policy before you "cry wolf"—you might be treading on sacred ground.)

S. The school is constantly pressuring me to improve my own education. (Avoid at all costs! Don't ever admit that you think you learned all you need to know— that's the extreme of presumptuousness. The school is asking you to invest in yourself.)

T. The student body has a deplorable school spirit. (Opportunity knocks! Here's your chance. Give them anything worthwhile and you will probably have all the students clamoring to get into your classroom. A sagging spirit is the result of "Lack of Pride" in anything with the school name on it. .Give them a champ!)

U. The rival school has a better program and the community would rather support them. (Join forces. Don't compete. Put all of the energies into cooperation. Create something where you and your group must work with the rival on a joint program. If they are better, you'll learn by example. If they aren't, you will have shared with a colleague and established a precedent for the future.)

V. My colleagues won't help by sharing any of their knowledge. ("Monkey see, monkey do." Enough said.)

W. My college didn't adequately prepare me to be a music educator. (There's a tremendous difference between knowledge and wisdom. Don't get caught in the trap of thinking one can replace the other. Let's hope our family physicians never blame their med schools for their miscalculations. This comparison points out the fault of this kind of reasoning.)

X. The fund-raising program takes too much time away from valuable rehearsal time. (If you are spending time counting oranges or delivering candles, you do need to check your time priorities. Part of any fine program is involving parents and students in these tasks. This reminds me of the band director who spent his whole music career (two years) working on his music library. The band couldn't play a B scale in whole notes, but he library was a showcase!)

Y. I'm personally just burnt out. (This can happen, does happen, and will happen. When did you last take a vacation? When did you last treat yourself to a really professional musical performance? When was the last time the band had a cookout? Played softball? When did you last thank everyone for their contributions? What was the last music convention you attended? When did you last play your own instrument? Change the pace, do something different, do anything! Don't continue to chastise your own value. "Burn-out" is a homespun label that indicates a one-way path to problems unless there is a change.)

Z. Our school custodian trains these carnivorous rats to chew off the tips of the fingers of my woodwind players! (Now there's a valid problem that needs immediate attention!)

We've exhausted the alphabet! If none of these apply to your own situation, check with your principal immediately: you may not be teaching music!

What this all says is: *everyone* has these problems. They are part of every school system in some degree or another. The successful people in the music education world go about solving them or they discover a way to work around them. It's easy to identify problems. Coming up with the solutions is another story. Energy spent complaining about circumstances is energy lost in correcting the same circumstances. "Argue for your limitations and you get to own them!"

*"Ability is rated by what is
finished, not what is started."*

# Action: The Key
# to Motivation

*"Motivation—where can I buy some?"*
   *"If the students would just focus all of their energies, then
we would have a great group."*
   *"They never seem to reach their full potential. Just one time
I wish they would all give 100 percent"*
   *"This year's group has so much talent, but we're having
an attitude problem!"*

Sound familiar? Ever made any of the above statements to
your colleagues? To your spouse? To *yourself*? It really doesn't
make a whole lot of difference if a group is blessed with oceans
of talent if they are not motivated to actualize it. An all-state
clarinetist with a full-ride scholarship to a music conservatory
can be a detriment to a program if his or her attitude is negative,
causing a cooperation/communication barrier. We can purchase
the finest equipment, recruit the most talented musicians,
create an outstanding parent support organization, set up a
European tour, commission a special work of music, bring in
one of the nation's finest conductors, and still have a group
with a negative attitude!

The truth is: We cannot give students motivation. (Most of us have to muster up our finest efforts just to create our own supply!) What we can do is set the example and point out "thinking habits" which will serve as a basis for having a positive attitude. As a result, people can choose to be motivated.

*"People behave according to how they feel, not what they know."*

Psychologists have told us this for years, yet many people continue to ignore this reality. When students "feel good" about themselves, they perform accordingly. (Unfortunately, the inverse of this "law" is also true: Low self-esteem produces mediocre-to-poor results.) In our haste to be outstanding music educators, we may have overlooked one of the "key" ingredients: creating a "good feeling" in rehearsals and performances.

Take a brief moment and remove yourself as "the director" of your group. Recreate yourself as a "new member" getting ready to spend your first day in "your" musical organization. Now walk into the rehearsal room. How does it make you feel? Does the room give a feeling of warmth and care? Do you feel as though you are in an environment which will ask for and support your finest effort? Do you and your fellow musicians sense that it is a place where you want to invest your time and energy?

Be careful not to confuse "neatness" with a "caring atmosphere." We have all been in rehearsal rooms that were so organized and clean they felt sterile. At the same time, there is a lot to be said for the security we all feel in "organization." Entering a rehearsal room which looks like the latest cyclone disaster is not a good launch for a great practice. In other words, part of a positive attitude can be handled by "setting the stage." The environment must be conducive to promote and exemplify your goals!

What is accepted behavior in this rehearsal room? We are all creatures of habit. Whatever actions we see around us, we tend to become: language, topics, focus, physical behavior, and yes, even attitude! We all reflect our environment. Therefore, if it is acceptable to practice "discus throwing" with a crash cymbal then it is obviously all right to destroy furniture, scar the walls, graffiti the practice rooms and use the director's office as a public dump. When energy is not focused, the options are limitless! *Do we motivate to support the "pride" or simply threaten to insure survival?*

How is the "attitude" of the director as you look through your new set of student eyes? Do you feel you are wanted? Do you feel you can really make a difference? What will be the reward for your attention and effort? Will you be recognized for what you contribute, or simply reprimanded for an error? Will you feel you were able to help the conductor? Were you able to add to the performance of the group, or are you just "filling a chair?"

How about the actual rehearsal? Did you learn anything? Was there a musical experience that made you feel good about your playing? Was there a feeling of cooperation and commonality with the other members? Did an attitude of "we/us" prevail as opposed to a selfish "I/me" attitude? Did you really "get into it" or were you just "hanging out" until the rehearsal was done?

When we allow ourselves the opportunity to mentally experience being in a group, solutions to the various motivational attitude problems become clear. In many cases, the problems really can be defined and, in turn, lead you to the solutions. It is difficult to find a solution when the problem isn't clear!

Only directors who really want the motivation of the group to be high will go through this sometimes painful process. It is a matter of self-evaluation which is threatening to anyone who is insecure. The very finest directors are constantly looking at their total rehearsal environment and making necessary adjustments to improve an already fine situation. Those people who don't want to meet the challenge simply "blame" the circumstances and spend fruitless energy defending the fact that their students "simply aren't motivated."

For most students, it's not a case of being unmotivated. Everyone is motivated. It's more a case of being motivated to put the energies where they will pay off. What is the payoff for practice, lessons, discipline, extra rehearsals, 100 percent effort? The trouble is that the rewards we can offer are intangible: pride, self-esteem, integrity, expression, family, care, serving, sharing. Our value system doesn't always recognize these rewards. In this day and age of instant gratification, we must compete with sports cars, fashion clothes, MTV, and that frightening peer pressure. With that in mind, we quickly see that part of the task at hand is the education of the value of intangible rewards. When we don't "live" with these values in our own lives, we quickly forget them. Our own energy becomes misdirected and the "I/me" philosophy takes over once again. "If you show me how happy a motivated/positive person is, I just might try it myself!" That could be a great payoff. It would motivate me!

Motivation comes either from fear or desire. More than likely, you are passing your own motivational source onto your students. We all know fear will work and is very effective for immediate results. It is also something that prepares us for traumatic experiences we will face in life. However, groups who work under constant fear tend to perform "in spite of" instead of "as a result of." Use fear motivation with great caution!

Desire, on the other hand, tends to remove "set limits." Through this, we open up a whole new level of personal creativity and all the benefits which come from being creative: self-expression, feelings of contribution, personal pride, high self-esteem, etc. "Motivation by desire" promotes the exact qualities that we are offering as a payoff for the student's commitment to the musical organization. Two plus two equals four!

Now let's go back to those original statements and see if we can come to some conclusions.

1. You don't need to buy any motivation: you've got all you could possibly want. It's just a matter of getting it focused in the direction that will produce excellence.

2. The art of focus is never complete: it is on-going. One must be on the lookout at all times to find one more place where there can be gain to add to the momentum. The worst thing to do is ignore it. Stay on it!

3. To get 100 percent effort from any group it is necessary to make people feel good about themselves. To expect several (sometimes hundreds) of students all to have a "joyous day" at the same time so they will perform a great concert is like betting against Murphy's Law. Hoping the good feelings will just happen is simply not a good use of hope. Be aware that society is bombarded with negatives, from television to our

own educational system. We have learned to survive on what not to do. Therefore, a major part of our teaching should include methods and processes which create good feelings. Yes, even for ourselves. We should feel good about our work. When you feel good, you give 100 percent.

We all have great potential, and we all have attitude problems. The most effective cure for a negative attitude is to create some kind of action; not only does it stimulate motion, but it also consumes the time which might be directed towards thinking about "how bad things are."

Potential that is not actualized cannot serve others, it can not create action. It is like having money in the bank but no way to withdraw it. When any group becomes dormant, it is a certainty that there is some kind of attitude problem. Without action to offset the attitude problem, it will perpetuate and usually get worse.

The formula is simple. Action causes motivation, which can create and actualize potential. Don't react, act!

Observe outstanding organizations and notice the common factors of success: busy schedules, constant preparation, a desire to refine and make things better, intensity in all facets of the operation, enthusiasm at all levels, a sense of "family" and group purpose, lots of action, lots of communication, even controversy, high levels of productivity, people who care!

Motivation is an exciting and necessary part of any musical group: It is the "oil that runs the machine" of progress and growth. Motivation is our greatest natural resource and the supply is endless., and more important, this wealth is available to everyone.

The key to bringing this quality to the forefront is within each of us and it involves a constant search for, and belief in, our own abilities. Not to accept this responsibility is a major violation of our right to live a happy and productive life. Our students deserve to see us at our best.

It's time to create a little action!

*"Happiness lies in the joy of achievement
and the thrill of creative effort."*
— Franklin D. Roosevelt

# The Price of Success

To date, I have not met anyone who did not want to be successful in whatever they choose in their life. Not many say, "I think I'll just be mediocre...it seems to satisfy my needs!" Yet there are people who seem to avoid success because of rather meaningless, shallow excuses. Why? Why would anyone settle for less than he/she can be? As teachers, do we not all have the obligation to serve as role models of and for excellence?

Is it that people don't want to be successful, or is it that we have not learned *how* to be successful? We certainly have an abundance of information which should "boost us to the top," however there are still countless examples of people who are not willing to take the risk of going for it. Yes, that includes both you and me.

What would you do if you knew there was no way you could fail?

Isn't that fun to think about? If you knew there was no way you could lose, be side-tracked, detoured, embarrassed, humiliated, or intimidated. If you knew you would forfeit nothing, but only gain and benefit, what would you do? Isn't it true that most of us have set limits on what we can do simply through self-inflicted barriers? Literally, our success is at the mercy of our own doing. We have the potential to do just about anything (and it may well be: anything!) we choose. Yes we do! To say, "Nah, we don't," is just more self-limitation. It is a matter of convincing ourselves (our self-image) that we are capable of going beyond our present-day limits.

In a brilliant anthology, author Anthony Robbins explains the way our mind works on electronic impulses (research done at Stanford University) where we can now identify the positive and negative impulses being sent via brain waves which dictate our behavior. Negative impulses cause negative behavior, and positive impulses cause positive behavior. The mind, much like a computer, simply processes the message and kicks back the behavioral patterns we are to act out. The mind cannot distinguish whether they are right or wrong, but merely acts upon the given data just as a computer would run whatever disk we inserted. The real exciting part is: *Our conscious mind has the ability to make the choice of whatever message we want to send*! In other words, we choose the program for our own behavioral computer.

When we don't consciously make this choice, the mind will simply take whatever is the loudest sensory information and use it as the computer program. It is like drifting aimlessly at sea when we have the ability to guide our ship, if we take the responsibility of steering it.

There is a "price to pay" for success, just as there is a price to pay for negative conditions. It is not a random "luck of the draw," but a systematic, self-disciplined plan of action which affords everyone the same opportunities for reaching his/her goals.

Not to over-simplify this formula, the reader can rest assured there are volumes written on the subject which warrant study, but the condensation of everything boils down to this three-step process: vision, commitment, action—or for those of us who understand "plain old language"—ready, *aim, fire.*

VISION (READY)—The people who "make it" have this in common. They see, dream, and envision their goal before it ever becomes reality. They burn it into their sub-conscious and can describe every detail of their dream.

Knowing the mind will always lead us in the direction of our most dominant thought, these winners make sure they are constantly reaching into their creative mind to shape/sculpt/ draw their exact blueprint of the future. They leave nothing to chance.

COMMITMENT (AIM)—Successful people understand "the world is not devoted to making them happy" and face the responsibilities of successful living, knowing it will mean sacrifice in certain areas. But they also understand the personal growth and strength which will result from this effort, which really makes it a benefit.

Anyone can succeed if they are willing to make a personal commitment to handle:

1. FRUSTRATION—Everyone experiences this through life.

2. REJECTION—Have you ever met a successful person who has not been subjected to rejection...*lots* of rejection? In fact, the really successful man or woman sees rejection as a chance to learn and grow.

3. FINANCIAL PRESSURE—Whether we like it or not, it is part of our society. The only certain way not to have any financial pressure is to not have any finances...and that, in itself, could be real pressure!

4. LACK OF WILL TO GROW—Complacency is a dangerous mood. It can cause the mind to rationalize everything from boredom to apathy. When skepticism appears, the "red flag of danger" should be bright in your vision. When we're convinced "we can't," we become our worst enemy on the road to success.

You must "take aim" through your personal commitment to follow through no matter what obstacles or barriers you encounter. Each disappointment can serve as a stepping stone in reaching the goal.

ACTION (FIRE!)—The last key element of the trilogy. It is easy to "dream the dream," and even exciting to sit down and "draw up the plan," but doing it, actually taking action, seems to be where many halt. If we are expecting people to come to us to support our endeavors, then we have missed the point. If your dream is not worth self-action, then what is its value to begin with?

"But what if I miss the target when I fire?" Reload and fire again! "But what if I run out of ammunition?" The fuel to fire your efforts is self-created and the closer you get to the goal, the more enthusiasm and excitement you will experience. Positive energy produces more positive energy (part of the Stanford research findings) just as negative energy produces negative energy. What is the basis of your energy source? Positive or negative?

It is important to see the order of the system: vision, commitment, action (ready, aim, fire!). If this order is violated, the formula loses its potency, and we all have examples of this in our lives. Don't you know many situations where you have seen something like this: ready, fire, aim. (It is important to have "aim/commitment" in place prior to firing. We might wound someone, including ourselves, by not having a good plan!

Then there is the case of the over-planner with this common pattern: ready, aim, aim, aim, aim, aim.... (These people do not want to "fire/take action" because they don't want that next level of responsibility.)

One of my favorites (self-recognition!) is the infamous: fire, ready, fire, aim, fire! (How many times have we all just wasted human energy in our fruitless attempts to get the job done! No plan, no vision, no goals, no organization, just blind uncontrolled energy being shot in a hapless, hopeless attempt to hit some unseen target!)

We can all play with the pattern and apply it to any situation. The humor is a catalyst that allows us to understand our errors. If we do not learn from them, we have destroyed the greatest worth of the experience.

The three-part formula is tried and true. It works. Use it!

Success (whatever it is for you, and it is different for all of us) is available in abundance to each of us in our daily work, personal lives, and missions in life. Our limits are exactly that: *our* limits! Using the "ready, aim, fire" technique for success seems like a small price to pay for making our dreams come true. Just take ten minutes out of your busy day to check yourself. Do you have your vision clearly in mind? Have you carefully established your committed plan of time and organization to get there? Are you taking action to achieve your goals?

What you will gain personally is exciting, but far more than that, you will offer your students a role model of endless, limitless possibilities! Let them buy into your success. That's a price-tag every student can afford, and will certainly want to purchase! It's a cheap price to pay for personal happiness.

FIRE!

> *"The spirit, the will to win, and the will to excel are the things that endure. These qualities are so much more important than the events that occur."*
> —Vincent T. Lombardi

# A Matter of Attitude

Attitude...it's a word we use a lot in our teaching world. It's become the "reason" a group does better, the "quality" which separates the winners from the losers, the generic term which defends every conceivable kind of behavior, and perhaps more than anything else, the one non-tangible all of us are trying to achieve, expand, create, share, and bring to the lives of our students.

We've all heard (if not said) these statements about this elusive attribute:

"This group is so talented, but you all have such a negative attitude!"

"The potential of this organization will never be realized unless we improve the attitude!"

"Our lack of success has nothing to do with all the problems we discussed. It is a matter of developing a positive attitude."

"You could have such a brilliant future, but first, you must develop a more congenial attitude."

Do any of these sound familiar? We do a lot of talking about attitudes, but when it comes to actually making any changes in the given behavioral pattern, there is a great deal of confusion. Where does our responsibility start and end when dealing with students (or parents, friends, colleagues) in terms of how they choose to behave?

There certainly is no question: the attitude of any individual, group, environment, etc., is the foundation for success. Students (anyone) with a positive attitude can make such a significant difference simply by exuding this quality via their presence. Everyone likes to be around bright, happy people. Unfortunately, the inverse is also true. Negative people can put a damper on the most festive event.

If we want to get maximum efficiency from our time and effort in rehearsals and performances (or anything else in life), it is vitally important to establish a positive, productive attitude. (Haven't you participated in those rehearsals, booster meetings, trips, etc., where it was a constant battle to maintain focus and attention?)

Knowing this, the obvious key to success in any endeavor is to be certain all those involved have a proper attitude. Simple! Simple concept, but most assuredly, a difficult task to pull off. Very difficult! It would be great if there were some magic pill we could give to everyone just before the practice that would ensure everyone's most positive attitude for the given time needed to accomplish the goal. (With a great attitude, it would probably even take less time than we had scheduled!) Dream on!

Some continue to use domination as a form of attitude control. This is effective, but demands an energy level which is certain to exhaust even the most energetic educator. (Results equal burn-out.) Then there are those who simply allow the students to be. This may work well for the highly motivated learner, but most students (and we) need focus and direction mixed with a generous portion of role model leadership.

Rather than be "at the effect" of our circumstances, perhaps there is some formula, some information which can help us to understand the workings of the attitudes of our students. Before we can have any impact on helping them develop a positive attitude, we must be aware of how these patterns are set in the first place.

PEOPLE BEHAVE ACCORDING TO HOW THEY FEEL. This psychological truth is the basis of any good teacher's secret to success. It's not "what we know," but "how we feel" which determines our behavior. Therefore, to have any effect on creating a high-learning environment, we must make certain the people are feeling good about themselves.

The next question is obvious: "How do I go about making people feel good?" Nobody can make anybody feel anything. This is where all of us have wasted a lot of time and effort. We all make a choice, each and every moment, which determines our feelings. Those who "feel bad" choose this for themselves. Likewise, people who "feel good" make the same choice in determining their attitude.

If we go back one more step, it is easy to see how this all comes about.

TRUTH 1: I CONTROL MY THOUGHTS. We all have the ability to put into our minds, at any given time, any thought we want. Nobody else makes that decision for us. We can be in an audience listening to a beautiful symphony, yet be out on the lake fishing in our minds. It's a simple choice guided by our wishes.

TRUTH 2: MY THOUGHTS CONTROL MY FEELINGS. It is impossible to have a feeling without a thought. Our mind has a thought and then computes and determines what our feeling should be. Thus, different people feel quite differently about the same situations. Feelings do not just happen, they are the result of a thought process.

TRUTH 3: I CONTROL MY FEELINGS! It's fairly obvious, through deductive reasoning: If I control my thoughts and my thoughts control my feelings, then—obviously—*I control my feelings*!

Once we have grasped this understanding, we can see that we can also control our attitude because *we behave according to how we feel*! Knowing this, we can take some control over our actions and not go through life being "Destiny's Plaything." It gives us some say-so about: who we are, what we do, how we can contribute to the world. Of course, this information affords us the opportunity of affecting the attitude of our students. They (we) must understand they have the responsibility for their own attitude...and, they can (and do) determine their attitude via the thoughts they choose to put in their minds.

In our modern day computer language, there is a common phrase, "Garbage in, garbage out!," What it means is that when we feed bad information into the computer, it will give us bad information back. The same thing is true when it comes to accepting responsibility for our attitudes. If we continue to feed ourselves bad thoughts, our behavior is destined to reflect the results of this information. When we feed ourselves positive thoughts, our behavior adjusts accordingly.

What could possibly be the advantage of feeding the mind negative thoughts which are certain to result in negative feelings, generating negative behavior? It simply does not make sense. Why would anyone abuse themselves like this?

Perhaps it's because we have relegated ourselves to thinking it's O.K. to be negative, and if we continue to behave with a high level of negative focus, someone will come to our aid and bail us out. (And the tooth fairy lives!)

As educators, we have such a responsibility to serve as a positive role model, demonstrating the epitome of a healthy attitude. Once the students see us do it and realize the many benefits which come to those with a good attitude, the desire to jump on the bandwagon will motivate them to "join the ranks."

Maybe attitudes are not such a mystery, but more of a result of responsibility!

Here's to positive thinking equals positive feelings equals positive behavior. Even this is a matter of attitude!

# Part Three

# Student Leadership

# Student Leadership:
# A Lifetime Study

If there is one specific area of attitude development where everyone wants help, it is certainly in the area of student leadership. It is a well known fact that "we can't go it alone," and the answer to having a successful program is in direct proportion to the effectiveness (or existence) of a powerful and productive student leader organization.

Until the early 1980's, I thought that meant delegating the various work assignments to people who seemed to have a specific talent in a given area. If they were successful, they either kept the job or were promoted to a more responsible position. If they were not successful, they were dismissed from their position and someone else was given the chance. However, there was never much direction concerning "How to Lead."

I wasn't using any of the techniques described in this book in my own leadership. What is even more frustrating, now that I have this information, is that it is obvious I could have saved many potential great leaders, but simply "gave up" on them in my own ignorance.

One of the basic laws of leadership centers around this universal truth: We can't improve our conditions until we are willing to improve ourselves. So many people want the privileges of leadership, but aren't aware of the added responsibilities which leadership requires. The honor of the title, the diplomatic favor of the management, the stage to make decisions and guide, are all wonderful, but one pays an expensive price for these positive additions to life. Therein lies the real trick to this whole leadership mystery.

Leadership really is a lifetime study. If we can help one person achieve a higher level of leadership skills, we have positively contributed to his/her life in the most powerful fashion imaginable. It is a gift they can use time and time again, and, more importantly, give to others which further multiplies the gift's value.

What is a leader? Let us begin this section of the book with a quote from Kathryn E. Nelson from the 1979 National Leadership Conference. It is tremendous and could easily find its way to your bulletin board for those who want to take the lead!

## A LEADER?

I went on a search to become a leader.

I searched high and low. I spoke with authority and people listened but alas, there was one who was wiser than I and they followed her.

I sought to inspire confidence but the crowd responded, "Why should we trust you?"

I postured and assumed the look of leadership with a countenance that glowed with confidence and pride. But many passed me by and never noticed my air of elegance.

I ran ahead of the other, pointing the way to new heights. I demonstrated that I knew the route to greatness. And then I looked back and I was alone.

"What shall I do," I queried? I've tried hard and used all that I know .

And I sat me down and I pondered long.

And then I listened to the voices around me. And I heard what the group was trying to accomplish.

I rolled up my sleeves and joined in the work.

As we worked I asked, "Are we all together in what we want to do and how to get the job done?"

And we thought together and we fought together and we struggled toward our goal.

I found myself encouraging the fainthearted. I sought the ideas of those too shy to speak out.

I taught those who had little skill. I praised those who worked hard .

When our task was completed, one of the groups turned to me and said, "This would not have been done but for your leadership."

At first I said, "I didn't lead, I just worked with the rest."

And then I understood: leadership is not a goal. It's a way of reaching a goal.

I lead best when I help others to go where we've decided we want to go.

I lead best when I help others to use themselves creatively.

I lead best when I forget about myself as a leader and focus on my group, their needs and their goals.

To lead is to serve. To give—to achieve TOGETHER.

# You Can't Go It Alone!
# C'mon Student Leaders!

One of the most popular conversations in our profession centers around the whole issue of stress. Are you aware the world of music ranks *second* in stress-related vocations? Now, you don't feel so bad, do you? It's true. The "pressure of performance" is one that puts the human body in an anxious state much of the time. As a result, we suffer a tremendous drop-out rate in our band-directing ranks. At last look, the average survival was a seven-year stint. A four-plus year investment in college is quite a gamble for such a short tenure of practice.

Although much of the struggle is emotionally self-inflicted—we are artists, you know!—this understanding does not remove the mental, emotional, and physical breakdowns often blamed on the vocation. It is as real as the common cold and the longer we ignore the problem, the more certain it is to infect (affect) our finest educators in the band world.

What's the answer?

Aren't you always amused at those fool-proof "pat solutions" which are so popular:

- *Get more balance in your life. (Are you kidding?!)*
- *Spend less time at your job and more time playing croquet.*
- *Don't take your work so seriously. What if the band can't sight read?*
- *Avoid being emotionally involved with your boosters even if they do threaten your home and your children.*
- *Ignore those wrong notes and that disgusting intonation, just close your ears and think of the rolling ocean during the incoming tide.*
- *If your administrator refuses to speak to you in the hall, simply "learn from the experience" and create a space of being.*
- *So you're overdrawn on your budget and cannot account for $4,000 in your uniform fund.—that's why there are school lawyers!*

This is analogous to telling an overweight person they need to be more careful about what they eat!

Yes, there certainly is a huge dose of sarcasm in all of this; mainly because our finest band directors all know these "answers," yet we continue to lose our most effective music educators to other careers because they simply burn out, wear out, give in, give out, and often just throw up their hands in a state of frustrated disbelief.

How can one work this hard, put in so much time and energy, have created such a positive program of success, and still have feelings of incompletion, lack of accomplishment, falling short, all neatly wrapped in a state of physical/mental exhaustion? (Have we not all experienced this at least once...each day?) Is there a way out of this seemingly vicious circle?

This article is certainly not going to offer you another "quick fix" solution, but it does have some pragmatic information which has been time-tested, and appears to be a common denominator among the "sane ones" in our market. It all revolves around *prioritizing* the work and *delegating* much of it to student leaders. This is certainly nothing new, yet it has some modern twists which could be very interesting to you. The ability to prioritize with some careful personal planning, and delegating with a responsible sense of management wisdom, can alleviate much of the undue stress which appears in many band rooms each day.

Do you ever catch yourself using your time and energy on a task which could be capably handled by a student leader? For example:

1. Stuffing and emptying music folders. (Certainly there must be some training, but a good student librarian can give you more time to study scores, or even play a round of golf, heaven forbid!)

2. Entering data into your band computer. (Let's be honest about this. Your hot-shot sophomore bassoonist knows more about that little baby than you will ever hope to understand, or are you just trying to brush-up on those dormant typing skills? For many, this can be an escape from the real responsibilities, instead of a task only *you* can do. Sorry, but true.)

3. Being the financial guru of the fund-raising project. (Money is a tricky thing, isn't it? Have you considered a two-man team including a band booster and an aspiring accounting major? To be harshly honest, they probably couldn't abscond with as much as most musicians lose based on the track record of our monetary-management prowess! This "rounding off" to the nearest hundred has got to stop!)

4. Serving as superintendent of ensemble properties—more commonly known as "straightening up the band room" which, for some, is not even on the "to do" agenda! (Haven't we all witnessed the dedicated-never-do-anything-wrong band director spending a faithful hour each day tidying up the rehearsal hall, while a group of upperclassmen stood by on the sidelines visiting about the latest Sting recording? You bet we have. A proud student band manager could probably do the job better, and it would free us/you to crank up the stereo system with a first class performance of "Candide" and maybe even share the storyline with those upperclassmen.)

5. Getting caught in the undertow of correspondence. *DON'T TRY TO BE YOUR OWN SECRETARY.* If you're good at it, you should become a secretary! Your time is too valuable to spend deluged in a mountain of paperwork. (With the limitless possibilities of most word processing programs and a hand-held tape recorder, you can create a magnificent "learning lab" for your second chair flute who has a full ride scholarship to the local secretarial college. Yes, you'll have to do some

training in this endeavor, but wouldn't it be nice, just for once, to keep up with your mail? And keep your second chair flute happy at the same time, even though she didn't win the challenge of the solo part?)

6. Now that you're "on a roll," let's not "take roll!" O.K., you get to do it during the first week of the semester to learn everyone's name, but this can be a mindless daily task which is an open invitation for the percussion section to commit acts of terrorism while you are searching out some student who didn't hear his name called in the first place. Lots of tutti long tone and warm-up chorales can be played during this common policy exercise.

And the list can go on (with appropriate cynicism authored within each explanation) forever. The point is: student leaders are available if we are willing to "prioritize" the daily goals and responsibly "delegate" these with appropriate direction. Certainly there will be some mistakes, and it won't be as good as if you had done it yourself, but isn't that the very essence of our educational system: learning by doing, correcting when something has failed, and participating in the ownership of the organization?

Band directing is changing with the times. We/you cannot "go it alone." There is simply too much to do. Learn to give it away so you have room to take in more, which you can then give away to create more space to understand even more, etc., etc.

The key words of course are *responsibly* and *appropriate*. And that is where the art of teaching takes over and the absolute answers are no longer apparent. This is not a solo gig, it is a band: a group of people united for a common purpose. This could be the start of something big! (Apologies extended...it just fit so well!)

Coda: Strangely enough, those directors who seem to follow this path are the veterans in our profession. They have survived the "seven year itch." Although they may not be void of stress, they do have control of it and can always focus their energies when necessary while avoiding undue trauma for the sake of attention. Their perspective is clear and clean, and they serve, as those who set the standards, by creating new learning opportunities for the students each day. And if you take a second look, you will always see (right behind their success story) a support group of student leaders ready and willing to carry out the next step in the positive growth of "their."

In reality, shouldn't we all *band together*? "Anyone for croquet?"

*"The things to do are: the things that need doing, that you see need to be done, and that no one else seems to see need to be done."*
— R. Buckminster Fuller

# Seven Myths about Leadership

We are privileged in our profession to have the chance to work with students of high-intention, more-than-average commitment, and a desire to go above and beyond the call of duty. Certainly there are exceptions to this, but for the most part, young musicians represent the "cream of the crop." (If you ever question this, trade places with an academic teacher for the day, and don't deceive yourself by trying this experiment with one of the honor's classes, get one of those required courses!)

There is exhaustive research identifying students of the arts as the leaders in our society. Their sense of discipline and persistence offer them some certain tools for success as they assume the responsibilities of their life.

After ten years of presenting in-depth leadership workshops for this select group, certain patterns have surfaced which are worth sharing, for it will aid as you begin your own leadership training with the students in your program.

One of the realizations which has come out of all this involves the countless number of myths so many young people have about the mysterious world of leadership. Before we can define or even teach what leadership is we must erase these false notions, otherwise we are simply pouring water into a glass which is already full.

(I spent almost four years in total frustration because after carefully administering the right information about leadership, I would find much of it was in vain because all the data was predicated on the assumption that "leadership truths" were not in conflict with any of the individual's own beliefs. Upon discovering the number of mis-truths many young people have, and the accompanying considerations, it was quite evident a lesson about "The Myths of Leadership" was an absolute necessity before the building process could begin.)

The explanation of Leadership Myths might be enlightening to you as well as the students. In fact, it will afford many of the people who would never consider themselves to be "leaders" to come forward and offer wonderful talents and skills that you would otherwise never know existed within the organization. This is truly a positive win-win benefit for all.

## THE COMMON LEADERSHIP MYTHS

1. LEADERSHIP IS A RARE SKILL. Although there are very few who choose to be leaders, it is certainly not a rare skill. More appropriately, it is a "rare attainment." Research has proven time and time again that leadership can be taught. Every student has the ability to become a leader in some area of the group.

Let us be quick to add that leadership is not to be confused with politics or popularity. Some of our greatest examples of effective leaders focus on people who started out at the bottom of the heap. If one is willing to "pay the price," the goal is within reach...no exceptions.

2. LEADERS ARE BORN. Society has glamorized the idea of the "born leader" via T.V., movies, and the popular "rags to riches" stories which serve as an inspiration for all of us. Leadership is not genetic. Although we look at certain people as having extraordinary communication abilities, these are

learned skills too. Those who carry the label "personality plus" work at this endeavor each and every moment until it becomes a positive life-style habit. If you are born, then you can be a leader, and that is about the only thread of truth in myth #2.

3. LEADERS ARE CREATED BY DRAMATIC EVENTS. We've been watching too many "Rocky" movies, it seems! All-star wrestling and roller-derby have also added to this falsehood. The red-nosed reindeer is a great story with a wonderful message, but needs to be put in perspective as we go about our day-to-day leadership responsibilities.

So many people say, "Well, the opportunity for me to be a leader just hasn't appeared yet." It won't! Most leaders get their positions through their persistent dedication to some rather mundane and thankless jobs. They do it with such a sense of excellence they are automatically promoted to take on more prestigious assignments. "Nose to the grindstone and out of the air!" 'Tis the road map to success.

4. LEADERS ARE AT THE TOP OF THE ORGANIZA-TION. This myth probably keeps many from doing what needs to be done because they do not feel they have the vantage (or advantage) to make a difference. We have come to think that a title or label somehow buys a higher level of understanding and makes decision-making easier and more accurate. Undoubtedly, it is a benefit to have a high profile if one is to lead, but certainly not a necessity.

Some of our most influential leaders in history were people who embraced their mission with personal enthusiasm and carved their own way to success. Ultimately, the true measue of a leader is determined by the degree of accomplishment rather than the political posturing.

5. LEADERS CONTROL. Unfortunately, we often envision the leader as someone who maintains strict control over each and every situation, not to mention the authoritarian attitude towards the people they are leading. We often find the leader is very much "at the effect" of some rather obscure circumstances, and certainly things aren't always to their liking, but they persist in their goal-driven efforts. There will be people who violently disagree with them, others who do not obey their

directions or delegations, yet the leader continues to move forward, demonstrating an undying commitment to complete the task-at-hand.

So often the word "control" implies: oppression, domination, coercion, and manipulation. It is important to remember that we only have control over one person: ourselves. If people are "forced" to follow another out of fear instead of personal choice, it is not leadership, but rather dictatorship. (And history clearly points out the predictable results of this negative hierarchy.) The one form of control all leaders execute is self-control.

6. LEADERS ARE CHARISMATIC. Certainly there are some leaders who are charismatic, and if you have "the gift," (the literal meaning of the word) then by all means you should weave it into your leadership style, but it is not a requirement.

Recent studies have led many experts to believe the ability to capture an audience (followers)— which we have labeled "charisma"—may be an extension of highly developed communication skills that can be taught when the creative side of the mind is unleashed through a series of mental exercises. In other words, we are going to be able to teach people to be charismatic, which may be no more than teaching people the confidence to express themselves with disciplined, enthusiastic presentation skills.

Even the great speakers have stage fright, insecurity blocks, and that proverbial nervousness. However, they press through the apprehension and take a stand. It's called leading!

7. POWER IS BAD. Power is only bad when associated with greed and selfish ambition. This myth has forced many to stand back when they have so much to offer the organization. They have heard so many people accuse others of "letting the power go to their head" that they won't take the risk of being put in that same light.

We can quickly sight many examples of great leaders judiciously administering power for the welfare of the people: i.e. Winston Churchill, Martin Luther King, John F. Kennedy, Gandhi, our great religious leaders.

And power does not necessarily mean control. Again, society has often associated power with tragedy and human suffering.

Though there are many examples of power abuse, there are an equal (if not more) situations where power has created a better world for man, including: electricity, laser energy, medical breakthroughs, and certainly the shift which we are experiencing in the quest for world peace. Truly, it is the way we use the power.

It is said 10 percent will achieve leadership status in their life. (A recent Harvard project has narrowed that small percentile to 5 percent.) Is it possible this figure is not larger simply because people are not choosing to be leaders? And, if that is so, are they not making this choice built on some misconceptions, preconceptions, and/or bad information about "what it takes?" Apparently so.

Teaching and explaining Seven Myths of Leadership might open the door of opportunity to many of your students. It is amazing how many of them have already given up any notion of ever being a leader because of their sincere belief in one of the above fabrications. Here is a chance to unleash a wonderful source of possibilities for your program and involve more "leaders" at a higher level of responsibility.

I am sure if you post this article on the bulletin board, you will have several students curiously reading its message to be followed by some thought-provoking conversation. Encourage this! It is healthy beyond measure. And, most importantly, it will build the self-image of that quiet student who has been avoiding any form of leadership because of a fear of "not having what it takes."

Everyone has a special gift. Sharing that gift with others is the key to enjoying its full value. And since we cannot lead others until we lead ourselves, it is time to make the most of our lives by removing the myths and taking the lead.

*"Success depends on the second letter."*

# About this Thing Called Leadership

Where does it start? What makes a leader? What kinds of things should we be addressing with our students? Why do some people lead while others follow? Is it something we can teach, or is it an inherent quality?

Where do enthusiasm and focus become one?

These questions, plus many others, are asked daily by all of us. Leadership is something we have all experienced and talked about, but few are willing to define and live out what it really means. We all (sort of) have our own version of leadership because we, as most others, have had to discover this special skill for ourselves

We are masters at teaching skills; however, we have avoided teaching the most basic of all leadership skills: people skills! Is there any doubt that the ultimate leader is the person who has the most proficient people skills?

So many of our frustrations concerning our own leaders are centered around their people skills. They may be well-trained in their discipline, but they cannot seem to deal with people. Certainly, the fundamental education in training any potential leader must deal with their people skills: attitude, communication, disposition, listening techniques, sensitivity to others, basic values, compassion, and—most important—a genuine concern for others.

We have saturated our learning world with techniques to develop greater proficiency in technical skills. (Is there much further we can go?) To continue improving our techniques is certainly no guarantee of quality leadership, by any stretch of the imagination. A leader is someone who must give, and we can only give what we have. If the leader does not have a feeling of positive self-worth, how can one expect the leader to develop this in others?

If the leader is spiteful, frustrated, anxious, or possesses a host of other negative behavioral patterns, it is certain this will pass along to the group regardless of technical proficiency. The attitude of a leader is of prime importance.

It is facetious to talk about time management, goal attainment, organizational skills, management style, etc., unless all of this is based on a solid self-image. It is analogous to building a house on quicksand. The group is destined to "live-out" the attitude of the leader they follow. Let us make sure the personal development of the leader is responsibly handled before expecting quality leadership of others. It is basic!

Our business world has had to come to grips with this reality in the last decade, and many require training programs for their management teams—not only for executives but for everyone who deals with people.

The reason for this is quite simple: it works! Let us be wise and learn from our friends who have discovered this reality.

If there was ever a profession where positive self-esteem should be an absolute requirement, it is in education. Yet we all know many of our colleagues who insist on approaching everything from a very negative vantage point. They refuse to admit the benefits of thinking positively.

(What an irony: positive produces positive and negative produces negative. As long as they are negative, everything around them reflects this. It's a vicious circle!)

For our chosen student leaders to generate a positive self-image, we, as teachers, must assume the responsibility to do the same. It is contradictory to think they are going to go "above and beyond the call of duty" when we are not willing to set the example.

*"When nothing seems to help, I go and look at a
stonecutter hammering away at his rock perhaps
a hundred times without as much as cracking it.
Yet at the hundred and first blow it will split in
two, and I know it was not that blow that did it—
but all that had gone before."*
—Jacob Riis

# Student Leadership:
# What They Must Know

Student leaders are a necessity if we expect to have
quality organizations. The day of the director "doing it all" is
simply a part of history. Although many people are adding
extra staff members to their program, it is still important that
students take on many of the responsibilities which are part
of a quality group. (The education which comes from this is
a real bonus to these "leaders" as they take on the various
responsibilities of life.)

Often, however, our enthusiasm about getting the extra
help—combined with the eager student's desire to have a
leadership position—can create a situation that results in confusion
and disarray. The teacher is forced to spend time "sorting
through" the problems caused by miscommunications, hurt
feelings, overstepped boundaries, bruised egos, irate peer

groups, false accusations, etc. Is it all worth it? Wouldn't it just be easier to forget all this student leadership stuff and do it yourself?

Although the temptation is often there to give up on this seemingly endless backlash of problems, we might want to take a closer look at our preparation of these young people for their given set of tasks. So often, student leaders are chosen based on who plays the best, who has seniority, who is most popular, who's mother is booster president, and on, and on. All of these "reasons" certainly have validity; however, the purpose of a leader is to lead. If the selected leaders do not have this ability, then the effort is fruitless. In fact, it is unproductive from every aspect and will cause digression instead of progression.

Many of these problems can be avoided if the student leaders have some guidelines. We have all experienced the student leader who simply is not motivated or assertive in handling the responsibilities. Conversely, there are those who are so aggressive they bulldoze everyone, including us. There are those who are "afraid of hurting their friend's feelings," and those who "have no sense of diplomacy."

There is no right or wrong way to lead. There are no strict rules since every situation demands a different set. But we can help student leaders with some general "do's and don'ts." This way, the leaders will have a head start accomplishing their goals and you will avoid the frustration of always "re-doing what was not done well in the first place." or "repairing the damage done by an immature misinterpretation of position."

First of all, when students choose to take leadership roles, they must understand this means giving up some privileges. They are now expected to deliver on all the assumed rules of their new position: to be on time (or maybe a little early), to be professional (they are now a role model), to have a positive attitude (their attitude is reflected in all of their followers), and to maintain a high standard of excellence (as they go, so goes their group). In most cases, they will give up some of their popularity. Jealousy runs rampant, and there are always those who think they can do the job better, or should have been the one selected, etc. This is part of leadership and to let them think the position will be all fame and glory is simply a gross misrepresentation of what lies ahead. Leadership is a lot of hard work and the privilege of doing the work is often the only

139

reward there is. To expect more will lead to certain disappointment!

With this in mind, it would seem advantageous to prepare these students mentally for what lies ahead. We must give them the tools to deal with their peers, adults, friends, and even us. When one becomes a student leader, the communication level adjusts. There is a higher level of expectation and a degree of greater confidentiality. If the "expectations" are not met or the "confidentiality" violated, the trust level needed to develop a good leadership style is destroyed.

Here are some guidelines for traits desirable in a quality leader. It can serve as a "check-list" for your existing leaders and as a good prerequisite for developing future leaders.

## CHARACTERISTICS OF QUALITY LEADERS

1. HIGH ENERGY LEVEL—Since leaders are often asked to "go the extra mile," it is important they have a high level of energy to maintain a busy schedule, to perform last-minute duties, and to be the hardest worker of their group. The followers rarely will out-work the leader. The leader sets the pace!

2. KNOW HOW TO LISTEN—Such an important "secret to success!" Not only is this important when taking instructions, but it is mandatory when working with others. Listeners are few in number, and we all appreciate someone who has time for us. A great rule for leaders: Keep you mouth shut and your ears and brain open!

3. EXUDE SELF CONFIDENCE—A role model is three to four times more of a teacher than a teacher. If the leader is to gain the respect of his/her followers, then self-confidence is a must. None of us wants to follow someone who lacks confidence. We want secure, assured leaders paving the way for us.

4. HIGH LEVEL OF INTEGRITY—Leaders understand the ultimate importance of truth. They will always use complete honesty as the basis for any and all of their choices. Any deviation of this will, ultimately, damage the group.

5. SENSITIVE TO OTHERS—Truly great leaders operate from a position of "we-us" rather than the popular "I-me." They are an integral part of their group. They constantly avoid a posture of "being above" the other people; rather, they put themselves in the follower's position and accommodate their needs. They sense the mood of the group, as well as of the individuals, and this atmosphere is of constant concern.

6. WILLING TO FAIL—Yes, they admit to being human. They are quick to admit their mistakes and equally as quick to correct them. They never push the blame on any unsuspecting scapegoat, but realize there is more strength in truth than in "looking right" at another's expense.

7. SENSE OF HUMOR—Although there has to be a disciplined focus on the goal, it is often necessary to "lighten-up" and allow the followers a chance to relax, laugh, and then get back in action. Humor and silliness are not the same. Humor supports forward motion while silliness restricts it.

8. THEY EXEMPLIFY OPTIMISM—They do not react with undo trauma to problems, but realize that within every problem lies an opportunity for growth and forward progress. They welcome problems as a chance to test their leadership and gain self-improvement.

9. AVOID COMPARISON GAMES—They realize that most comparison stems from insecurity. Their goal is not to "be better than someone else," but to "be the best they can," thus allowing their group to be the best it can. Competition turns into cooperation and all "competitive spirit" is used to improve the situation for everyone.

10. CARING AND SHARING—They will never hurt intentionally, even though they understand there will be times when individual wishes will be overlooked in favor of their group's welfare. They understand that part of leadership is "taking some of the heat" for those unpopular decisions and they accept this responsibility with strength and dignity. Their sense of caring is ultimate and their willingness to share every ounce of talent and ability is top priority in their actions.

Is that all? Of course not, but it is a healthy beginning to outstanding leadership. If these ten attributes were a certainty for all of our student leaders, the rest of the task at hand would be simple. We have created a framework for the best, and any leader worth his/her salt will want to be the best. Isn't that why they wanted to be leaders in the first place?

Student leaders are an important part of any first class organization. Our position as band directors offers us a rare opportunity to create a living lab for these special young people who are willing to go above and beyond the call of duty. Let's get them started on the right foot (or the left foot for marching bands).

Take the lead in teaching them what it is all about!

> *"The people who get on in this world*
> *are the people who get up and look for*
> *the circumstances they want, and, if they*
> *can't find time, make them."*
> —George Bernard Shaw

# Real Leadership:
# What It Takes

This article goes out to all of those young people who wish to be leaders. Probably everyone is going to say, "That's me. I want to be a leader, to have everyone look up to me, to be important, to be able to tell other people what they should do, to have others be envious of my position. Yep, I want to be a leader. How can I do that?"

To begin with, many people get leadership and politics mixed up. Being a leader is much different than being a politician. If you want all of those things described in the first paragraph, I suggest you try politics. But if you want to be a leader, it is going to be a long haul, and it won't be easy. Lots of people say they "want to be a leader," but there are only a choice few who actually achieve this very special title.

We often think we can read a book and it will give us all the answers. Not true! We can learn some concepts about what it takes to be a leader, but every situation is different and the true leader  must be able to take the concepts and apply them to the specific situation at hand. Therein lies the secret: Can you take what you know and apply it to whatever circumstances happen? As you can see, real leaders have to be very flexible.

The easiest part about leading is getting the job. Whether it's as a drill team captain, drum major, pompon captain, band president, or whatever, being elected or appointed to these positions carries with it a lot of excitement and roaring congratulations for the victory. Then, the trouble starts!

First of all, you are confronted with people who thought they should have received the position and didn't. Then you have all of their friends to contend with. Soon your own friends may begin to pull away and resent the position of authority you have attained. Are you prepared to handle this kind of damaging jealousy in your life? The "glory" will certainly not offset the hurt. Here is your first chance to show that you're a leader. Move forward knowing this is part of what every leader experiences. Chin up. Move forward!

Next...your "assigned authority" will diminish in effectiveness. You may delegate some things to be done only to find they were never carried through as per your orders. When you question the person about the lack of follow-through, you might well be told in no uncertain terms what you can do with your position, your authority, and your stupid assignment! *Having a title doesn't make you a leader.* With your hallowed title and a quarter, you can't buy a coke! Your job is "to lead," not to be a dictator of unquestioned power.

What you may find happening is "a sense of feeling alone." It may seem that nobody understands your predicament and what you are going through. Talking to people about the situation won't make any difference and it will be so tempting just to "cash it in." Let someone else do all this leadership stuff!

There is no question that the position of leader has been over-glamorized to the point of non-reality. Our society has given the impression that leaders are given special privileges, are exempt from many menial tasks, and are constantly in the spotlight of fame and fortune. Nothing could be further from the truth! Leadership involves "giving." It is about doing for others. It is based on making "we-us" more important than "I-me." It is about wanting to be excellent regardless of the price.

Although there are no carved in stone rules about leadership, there are some concepts which seem to be common to all people who succeed at this task of helping others through their efforts. (Which ultimately improves the life of the leader.) For those people who truly want to take on this job, here are ten thoughts about the attributes of leaders, whether they are leading a country or a squad of four people in their marching band.

1. REAL LEADERS are also DOERS. Not only do they help direct the efforts of others, they are willing to get their own hands dirty. These are the people who come early and stay late, and they can always seem to find "one more thing to do" to make it better for the whole group. They lead by example!

2. REAL LEADERS always have time for others. Although they may have an extraordinarily busy schedule, they can always find time to squeeze in one more responsibility to help out the group or a friend. They display a sense of "anti-selfishness" which is without fanfare. They care!

3. REAL LEADERS are quick to identify mistakes, but they spend little time talking about them; rather, they go about setting a plan to correct the mistakes and do something about the situation. They always look upon failure as an opportunity to correct and improve.

4. REAL LEADERS do not spend any time criticizing others. They use their energies to help those around them. They never exclude, but are always willing to include.

5. REAL LEADERS avoid put-downs and sarcastic remarks which can wound other people. There is no attempt to make themselves look better by making others look worse. In fact, they are constantly looking for ways to compliment those around them and build common self-respect.

6. REAL LEADERS never strike back or try to "get even." Even though they are susceptible to pain, they refuse to hurt another person in an attempt to even the score. They see blame and revenge as wasted energy. Therefore, they move ahead rather than dwell on the negative.

7. REAL LEADERS "share" rather than "compare." They see competition as a chance for self-improvement and know the only person they are really competing against is the person in the mirror. They accept others for who they are and support them in becoming better.

8. REAL LEADERS accept the reality of peer pressure, but do not give in to the threats of "not being one of the gang." They understand that their integrity is the foundation of their present and future growth and they pride themselves in being a self-thinker.

9. REAL LEADERS never attack anyone or purposely hurt another person. They understand that we always end up hurting ourselves when we choose to attack another.

10. REAL LEADERS always go the extra mile. When others have given up, quit, or rationalized an easier shortcut, the real leaders are on the job, getting it done. Yet when the awards of championship are passed out, they are always in the background applauding everyone else.

As one can see, the demands for being a great leader are extreme. It's certainly not all spotlight and glitter. Yet, the personal satisfaction which comes from doing the job is of immeasurable value—and it will always lead you to a new and bigger challenge.

It is so much easier to join the masses and complain about everything than it is to roll up your sleeves and do something about it. Yet, we all know, regardless how much fussing and fuming we do, eventually, it is all going to come down to: getting on our feet and taking on whatever task lies ahead. *The real shortcut is to jump in and do it!*

There are many times when we don't want to be responsible. It is so much easier to blame someone for the circumstances than to go about making the situation work; yet, this is the one quality evident in all great leaders: The ability to stay in there until the job is done. They take on every task with a sense of purpose and caring for those around them. They are not smarter, more talented, or luckier than anyone else. They just don't give up!

Let me conclude this article with a challenge: A challenge for you to meet the requirements of being a real leader.

A student of mine shared this bit of wisdom with me. It was during a time of personal strife because many of the decisions I had to make as a real leader weren't very popular. I was down and about ready to give up. And then he shared this knowledge with me. It travels with me everywhere, and perhaps it will help you see how important it is to never quit.

## THE PENALTY OF LEADERSHIP
author unknown

In every field of human endeavor, he that LEADS must perpetually live in the light of publicity. Whether the leadership be vested in man or product, ENVY is always at work.

In Art, in Music, in Industry, the reward is widespread recognition—the punishment—fierce denial and detraction.

When one's work becomes a standard for leadership, it also becomes a target for the shafts of the envious few. If the leadership is mediocre, he will be left severely alone, but if it is of great value, it will set a million tongues a-wagging.

Jealousy does not protrude her forked tongue at the LEADER who is common. Only if your work is stamped: QUALITY will you be subject to slander.

Long after the REAL LEADERS have accomplished the task, those who are disappointed or envious continue to cry out, "It cannot be done!"

The REAL LEADER is assailed because he is the LEADER, and the effort to equal him is merely ADDED PROOF of that leadership. Failing to equal or excel, the follower seeks to depreciate and to destroy...but only confirms once more, the LEADERSHIP of the one he strives to defeat.

There is nothing new in all of this. It is as old as human passions. Envy, fear, greed, ambition, and the desire to surpass...and it all avails nothing.

If the leader truly leads, he or she remains the leader. That which is great makes itself known no matter how loud the clamor of denial. The real leader wins...always!

*"Until one is committed, there is hesitancy, the chance to draw back, always ineffectiveness. Concerning all acts of initiative, (and creation) there is one elementary truth, the ignorance of which kills countless ideas and splendid plans: that the moment one definitely commits oneself, then providence moves too, all sorts of things occur to help one that would have never otherwise occurred. A whole stream of events issues from the decision, raising in one's favor all manner of unforeseen incidents and meetings and material assistance, which no man could have dreamt would have come his way.*

*I have learned deep respect for one of Goethe's couplets:*

*Whatever you can do, or dream*
*you can, begin it.*
*Boldness has genius, power, and magic*
*in it.*

—W.H. Murray from
*The Scottish Himalayan Expedition*

# Leadership Purpose

Reminding yourself of your own purpose for being a leader helps you stay on track throughout your daily activities. A purpose gives meaning and importance to what you are doing. Examining purposes and keeping them in mind supports leadership.

1. PURPOSE. Everyone has untapped potential. Becoming a leader is a lifelong process. Purpose does not prescribe a final destination; it suggests a direction of growth and learning. It is impossible, for example, to arrive at a destination called "east." Traveling east makes more sense. We can use this purpose like a point on a compass and continually monitor our progress.

2. PROVIDE AN OPPORTUNITY. The American Heritage dictionary defines "teach" as: "To cause to learn..." "Cause" is defined as: "A person or thing responsible for an action or result." Since everyone is responsible for his/her own learning, no one else can be the source or cause of that learning. So we have an interesting dilemma. No one can cause another's learning and teaching is causing another's learning. There is only one possible conclusion. Teaching is impossible!

Don't be discouraged. Leadership as a profession is not in jeopardy. Even though teaching is impossible, leaders have an incredibly challenging and useful job. They provide an opportunity for others to learn. They can invite others to learn. Leaders set the stage in the most effective way possible for learning to take place. The responsibility rests with the individual.

Learning, defined as "the act of gaining knowledge or skill," is not only possible, it is the most natural act humans perform. It begins before birth and continues at least until death.

Leaders are responsible for providing an opportunity. The individual is responsible for learning.

3. LEARN AND ADOPT. Knowing what is needed to be successful is not enough. Unless strategies for success are put into action, they are useless. Leaders must not only learn, but also adopt methods to be successful in life. This often requires behavioral change. Selling leaders on the idea of changing their behavior is the ultimate challenge. Shifts in attitudes, values, and beliefs accompany shifts in behavior.

4. SUCCESS IN LEADERSHIP. There is no one model of leadership success that is appropriate for everyone. People are different and so are their pictures of success. Success needs to be defined individually by each unique leader.

## LEADERSHIP PHILOSOPHY

The underlying philosophy is based on three assumptions. They are:

1. There are no secrets.
2. There are no victims.
3. There are no solos.

1. There are no secrets. It is usually a mistake to assume that leaders are prepared to adjust to drastic changes in their environments and lifestyles. Assuming they know how to lead and how to be effective followers is also often a mistake. Being a leader for many years is no guarantee that you have mastered the process of leadership!

When talking to leaders who have dropped out, we discover that most leaders took the position with both the ability and the motivation to succeed. What they lacked was a clear understanding of the specific strategies needed to get the job done.

There are no secrets about how to be a successful leader. Anyone who can read a paragraph and follow simple direction can succeed in leadership. The path to success is clearly mapped. It is rarely a question of fundamental ability or motivation. More often it is a question of a leader being aware of effective strategies, experimenting with them, finding the ones that work for him/her, and adopting them as habitual behavior.

This material will demonstrate how to become a positive and appealing image of a successful leader. Almost anyone can identify with it. Once a leader sees that there is no secret or magic associated with being successful and begins to identify with a successful image, a powerful thing happens. The daily activities and performances begin to fall into alignment with this self-perception. This is more than halfway to his/her goal of becoming a master leader!

2. There are no victims. Blaming, whether we are blaming other people, ourselves, or circumstances, does nothing to empower us to get what we want in our lives. YOU CREATE IT ALL! (Both good and bad, leadership is Total Responsibility!)

3. There are no solos. We are social animals. Peer pressure is a major force in our lives. Others play a powerful role in

the development of our values, belief systems, and behaviors. A supportive environment, which includes positive support groups, is a critical element of leadership success.

# Part Four

# For Band Directors Only

# For Band Directors Only

W hen I'm on a plane and someone asks, "What do you do for a living?" My answer is always, "I'm a band director." Once a band director, always a band director.

Although it has been several years since I spent time in the classroom, I still spend each day teaching, directing, listening, learning, and an infinite number of things eliminate some of the incompetence which seems to be growing instead of diminishing.

Through the school of hard knocks, there have been some pretty great experiences which have brought forth data which could be of help to you, your band, your colleague, or maybe that young aspiring musician who is eager to become a music teacher extraordinaire. Every time I did something that worked, it was important to document it and pass it on to those innocent students in "Band Rehearsal Techniques 101." Hopefully, it would allow them to bridge this part of the educational process and focus their energies in other areas of the mystery.

The following articles are about the real stuff in the world of band directing. All the platitudes in the universe will not substitute for the discipline of simply getting the job done. We can philosophically espouse forever, yet someone has to do the hands-on teaching which, in reality, is the only way the band is ever going to develop any kind of excellence.

There are volumes written on everything from breath support to blending the overtone series with fresh fruit from Florida. Here are a few shortcuts which have been field-tested. If you want more—and you should—it is time to open the library of information available to us, and written by the genius teachers who have contributed much to our art.

As we all know, the greatest education started the first day of that first job. Then, and only then, our learning began to produce dividends. One of my greatest educational experiences happened during that first year of teaching and, with your permission, it will make the point better than countless paragraphs of argument. So here's the truth:

It was just before the first performance of the band, and with only four rehearsals left, the reality that the band sounded horrible was beginning to ring true. Following a particularly brutal rehearsal when I placed the responsibility on the band, and withstood appropriate counter-attacks from the angry musicians, I walked to the office with my head down, afraid to face the students in the hallway. Slumped at my desk chair, I simply began to weep; the pressure was just more than my narrow and inexperienced shoulders could bear. A veteran colleague walked by and observed my hopeless condition and asked, "What's wrong? Did someone die?"

"No," I snapped back, "I just went through the most miserable rehearsal of my life. l wasted time we had to have, embarrassed students who have been wonderful all semester, and made a royal *#$# out of myself. And, to top it all off, the band is going to sound horrible on Thursday evening."

"So?" he calmly asked, "What's the big deal? It's nothing new, we all go through this just before a performance."

"They didn't tell me about this in college," I whimpered. "All I ever wanted to be was a band director!"

He walked over, put his hand on my shoulder and chuckled, "They never do tell you about this. If they did, nobody would ever finish music school. And you know what else, Lautzenheiser? You are a band director—and you're gonna be a good one. So go clean your face, apologize to those kids who are still hanging around the halls, and for heaven's sake, call some extra rehearsals; the band sounds horrible."

l had to laugh to keep from crying harder. And he was right. And we did have extra rehearsals.

And in the end, although it was no Grammy Award winner, it was a very respectable presentation—due to the fact that my colleague gathered several other faculty members and sat in during the last three rehearsals and the concert. Miracles do exist.

Here's to the world's greatest profession.

*"Things to do are: the things that need doing,*
*that you see need to be done, and that no*
*one else seems to see need to be done."*
— *R. Buckminster Fuller*

# Special Thoughts
# for Your Band

Several years ago one of my favorite students gave me a little book for Christmas. It was entitled *Think* by Dr. Robert Anthony. It was full of beautiful sayings, wise thoughts, and vignettes of information which we all know, but ignore in our daily lives. After many readings, the book was passed to another friend, then another, etc. Although it only takes a few minutes of reading time, the wealth of personal readjustment which comes about as a result of this reading is immeasurable. Needless to say, the value of sharing it with students is equally as positive.

Six months later, a cancelled flight at the Durango airport gave me some unexpected browsing time in a local bookstore and lo and behold, another little book was on the shelf with the same unique cover, but a different title: *Think Again*, again by Dr. Robert Anthony. Three dollars later, more knowledge surfaced because of a few short pages of quick reading, refreshing reading, enjoyable reading, and sometimes uncomfortable and challenging reading. Certainly, another fine learning experience had taken place.

Either sales were good, demand was high, or both, for now there is a third mini-volume, *Think On*. And, as always, the reader can count on enjoying an eye-opening jolt, for each quote can be tailored to the specifics of every individual's life.

Now what does any of this mean in terms of band directing? Absolutely nothing. It is about the person and the growth and nurturing which is a life-long process. Now *that* has something to do with being a band director. It seems that each page could become a "Guide for a Better Day of Teaching," if not a reminder of our predictable human flaws and the purposelessness of defending them.

As you complete these last few months of school, it might be worth putting some of these up on the bulletin board when the appropriate moment is at hand. Many people read them, a choice few understand them, and some improve their life-patterns because of them. They will have a positive impact, guaranteed.

SUCCESS IS JUST A MATTER OF LUCK. ASK ANY FAILURE.

Although there is a bit of sarcasm here, it does point out that so many students are quick to blame everyone or everything for their plight. When we blame, we give up our own power to change and make things better. Those who are consistently successful have achieved this level by being committed to high standards and a strong work ethic. There are no short cuts. The fable of the tortoise and the hare explains more than who won the race, but who always wins the race. Good luck is much like a good crop; we harvest what we plant. Successful people are constantly investing for future returns.

YOUR POWER AS A PERSON IS MEASURED BY YOUR ABILITY TO COMPLETE THINGS.

We all get excited about something new, fresh, different, with many personal promises to make this project the ultimate of our efforts to date. Whether it is a new beginning to the school year, a new professional model instrument, a new folder full of music, or even a new chair-placement in the band; there comes with it a characteristic pledge commonly associated with the New Year's resolutions. That is certainly the easy part of the growth process: promises are easy to make, difficult to keep. "Follow-through" delivers the highest benefits of any human quality. Your worth—or self-worth—is in direct proportion to your completion quotient.

## IT IS EASIER TO TALK THE TALK THAN TO WALK THE WALK.

Everyone knows the path to ultimate success. Few are willing to make the journey. Lip service runs rampant in our society. Anyone can tell you how it should be done, but only a chosen few are willing to pay the price of delayed gratification and personal sacrifice which are a prerequisite for success. And it has nothing to do with talent, intelligence, or good fortune; it is the development of one's self-discipline to meet a high standard of excellence in each and every facet of life. Or as one of my band director friends said to his organization in an anxious moment, "If you spent as much time and energy practicing as you do talking, our band would win a Grammy every year!"

## IT IS MUCH EASIER TO KEEP UP THAN TO CATCH UP.

Procrastination is not part of any individual's success-pattern. Free time is carefully woven into the schedule out of choice while prioritizing the tasks which need to be accomplished. Those who play "catch-up" and are always behind tend to give up in moods of frustration. Putting off today what you can do tomorrow is a one-way street leading to low self-esteem. Commit to being committed, or give up giving up.

## SUCCESS MEANS GETTING YOUR BUT OUT OF THE WAY.

Every time we are tempted to counter with "Yes, but" we violate the value of the growth-step. For example, "We want the band to perform better, but we don't want to spend more time practicing." Within the statement is a lie which brings us right back to talking the talk and not walking the walk. Here is the truth: for the band to improve, the practice standards must go up. The choice is before us. There are no buts about it.
- Practice standards up = Better Band
- Practice standards down = Worse Band.
- Practice standards the same = Same Band

It is now time to vote. Let's remove all the buts! Putting these thoughts up on the band room wall is certain to draw some reaction, and perhaps even some action. If it hits close to home, it might be a gentle way of allowing those less-than-desirable habits of some to be self-adjusted. If someone makes a negative comment about them, it could be a case of, "if the shoe fits." The real benefit will come from that quiet student who never says anything, but patiently reads every word and then thinks about it in those moments of solitude. Once again, you have educated.

If nothing else, pick up a copy of the three little books. They will provide wonderful food for thought. Thought plus Emotion create Conviction. Conviction creates Reality.

Keep making a positive impact on your students through music. Strike up the band.

*"Ships don't come in; they're brought in."*

# Be Responsible for the Greatest Show on Earth

Attention all band directors. This article is guaranteed to give you all the answers on how to be a successful band director—the secret ingredient, the magic potion, the one-and-only, never-fail key to success. Here it is, all wrapped up in one neat little word: responsibility. (This is not meant to be a joke—just read ahead and see where you fit in). You have to be willing to take any set of circumstances and turn the given situation into bandorama heaven. At times, the negatives seem to so far outnumber the positives. It is easier to give up, or worse, just tread water. There's not a band director in this country who does not face a new set of problems each day, and the successful ones continue to produce excellent programs year after year. What special knowledge do they have that insures this kind of predictable success? What is it about their personalities that leads them to always have everything handled? The answer is: they understand responsibility and they know what kind of effort is needed to accept it and respect it.

There have been countless articles written about solving every conceivable problem that the band director encounters, from developing the double reed section to soothing the temper of an irate band booster. This very chapter is jam-packed with priceless suggestions that are certain to benefit any program—yet the problems still continue to mount, and the more you manage to solve, the more there seem to be. Band directors are constantly asking themselves this age-old question: "Is there an end to all of these obstacles and situations that keep the band from attaining the level that I want?" The answer is, No—it will never end, and having a great band program means taking on the entire responsibility for everything that affects the band. It is important to know the alternate fingerings that facilitate the technique of a fast woodwind passage and equally important to be able to:

1. convince 150 enthusiastic bandsmen to hit the sack at 10:30 p.m.
2. explain to the math teacher why the solo trumpet player must be absent from the weekly test
3. motivate a group of band parents to sell a truckload of oranges, or
4. stop the nosebleed from an over-executed left flank.

It's being a kaleidoscope of personalities and having the ability to adapt yourself instantly to whatever expert you must be at any given moment to solve the problem. (How fast can you shift gears?) You must give up your position about what you think (or have been told), a band director should be, or should do, as well as should not be, or should not do—simply do whatever is necessary to clear the way for the progress of the organization. When you become too good to take on certain tasks, you will quickly find that the band members have become too good to respond to your directions. The group of young people that you face every day is a direct reflection of your feelings and attitudes about your job. (Read that sentence again.) If you find that they: lack motivation, lack discipline, seem not to care, don't inspire you, and a host of other things, you will find the solution to all of these problems by looking in the mirror. The answer to every problem that faces your band is ultimately your responsibility. When the day comes that you don't solve the problem, it will grow and begin cropping up in other parts of the program.

Problems don't disappear; all forward progress stops when they are not solved. Band directing is not a pass-the-buck business: the buck stops with you. You *are* the band. As soon as you accept this responsibility, you'll find that improvement and success of your band is immediate. The longer you resist assuming this responsibility, the more you deny yourself the pleasure and fulfillment that makes band directing the most exciting and rewarding position in the field of education.

Commit your energies to giving equal weight to all the rights as well as all the wrongs; see the glass as half full, not half empty; allow your bandsmen to share the responsibility when the going gets tough; meet every situation head-on, and know that when you do this, there will be an army of young musicians ready to give you all the support you could possibly want and need. True leadership is a priceless commodity, and it comes from the experience of solving problems—not identifying problems. Unfortunately, there's not an encyclopedia for the modern day band director's problems; and there never will be, because when you lead, it means you have no one to follow. Quit searching for the answer; the answer lies in spending all your efforts in taking care of business and not wasting any efforts on crying about business. Let's take a common problem: the 3rd clarinet section can't play the contest music. You can:

1. Hope that they will learn the part, or
   a. have a weekly sectional
   b. assign each one a play-off time by a certain date
   c. plan a practice session with all the 1st clarinets assigned to teach the 3rd clarinets
   d. bring in a local college music major to work with them
   e. take all of them to the local college for a sectional with the clarinet teacher
   f. trade a sectional with the neighboring band director who was a clarinet major
   g. have special one-to-one sessions with the junior high directors
   h. rewrite the parts to accommodate the proficiency of the players
   i. offer special acknowledgment to the whole section when they accomplish the task before them and on, and on, and on.

There's no magic powder to sprinkle on them to produce the results. There's no clarinet wizard hiding in the band room who will teach them how to play while you hide in your office. There's no educational tool that can remedy all the problems with one genius stroke. There's you. And you have the responsibility to create a way for those 3rd clarinets to solve their problems and enjoy the contributions they can make to the entire musical score. If you spend your day hoping your band will improve, you are spinning your wheels—hoping will teach you only how to continue hoping to continue hoping to continue hoping (you could end up spending your entire career becoming a professional hoper). Don't wait, help never comes; simply open your eyes and do what you have to do and see it as allowing yourself to grow richer and richer. You will be amazed how much frustration can be avoided and how much joy and awareness can be gained by a total commitment to yourself and the people around you.

As a band director, you are part of the greatest show on earth and it's happening right here and now. The only way to enjoy the show is as a participant—so, go for it. If it sometimes seems that talking about the problem is easier than attacking the problem, check your problem evaluator. We all know many people who can talk a good band program, and the people who have fine band programs seldom have time to talk about them—the music speaks for itself. You are one of an elite group of people who can contribute significantly to a young person's life via a language that knows no barriers—what an opportunity! You can make a difference in this world by allowing your band to see that assuming total responsibility generates success and they in turn can apply this sure-fire recipe to everything they tackle in life. Now you know the secret ingredient; the magic potion; the one-and only, never-fail key to success. It's your responsibility to create the greatest show on earth!

*"There aren't any rules for*
*success that work unless you do."*

# Negotiation and Education: A Question of Balance

How many times have you heard statements like this: "That was the finest rehearsal that I've ever been a part of..." (Band members); "Thank you for all the extra work with the band...you give us far more than we could ever possibly deserve." (Band Officers); "Even though the budget is overdrawn, I want you to go ahead and purchase everything that you need...our band deserves nothing but the very best." (Principal); "We want to let you know that you have our full support in any extra rehearsals that you want to call; we understand the need for on-the-spot decisions that mean extra hours and extra trips to and from school for our sons and daughters . . ." (Band Parents); "Your band was far superior to ours. There's no doubt that you should have come out ahead of us in the competition" (Fellow Band Director); "Dear, I realize that everything at school needs your constant attention right now. Why don't I come in and work with you this weekend as you get ready for the second semester?" (Wife/ Husband).

Have you quit laughing? The point is this: you can be the world's greatest musician and a conductor *par excellence*, but neither of these mean that you will be a happy, successful band director, because the majority of the working day is spent negotiating situations which have little or nothing to do with musical standards. The mortality rate in the band directing profession is really astounding. So many aspiring young teachers are constantly trying to cope with tremendous frustration and anxiety simply because they are not prepared to deal with the organizational situations that are a prerequisite for a fine band program. There are certain professional hazards that are present in any group effort or activity; they cannot be ignored, will never disappear, and if not dealt with in a knowledgeable manner, they can cause the leader—the band director—to consider the entire life-style not worth it. Accept these facts:

1. Students will be appreciative but never completely satisfied with everything. It will either be too difficult, or too simple, or take too much time, or not be as good as the rival school, or be unfair in some respect—etc., etc., etc. Realize that you can't keep everyone happy all the time. Just enjoy the times when there is harmony in the group and deal with each individual problem as it appears. It's important not to ignore the students' suggestions or complaints, but keep them in perspective. Always be honest in your explanations and reasonings. It's their band, not yours. Don't let a wise-crack or a misunderstood comment turn your day into a disaster. Keep smiling!

2. Be aware that your principal is just another person who is trying to deal with his own problems. He is fighting a war on all fronts and often your aggressiveness is really the last thing he wants to deal with. I know, I know: that's his problem. True—but it doesn't change the fact that you're not getting your way. Temper tantrums are really a futile attempt at personal satisfaction, often doing more harm than good. Nobody's budget is adequate; no band director gets the salary he or she deserves; no program gets the attention that it warrants. Accept it: yours is not a unique situation. Everyone has to make compromises. Though you may be the most creative person in the whole world, and you may be the musical genius of the decade, to your principal you may very well represent another snag in his or her list of problems. Accept "No" with a smile and go on to your next set of goals. Pouting, sulking, griping, back-biting, and threatening are all sure ways of making you miserable, along with everyone you come into contact with—it's just a part of it. Don't waste your energy trying to repair the past, or proving that you were right. Move ahead, march on; shift your emphasis for the good of the program;

put on a happy face: keep smiling.

3. Band parents were not created to serve as slaves for the band. Hard to believe, isn't it? They have mastered the technique of finding fault with anything and everything that they do not particularly like. Here are some familiar examples:

a) Band parents meetings that conflict with Monday night football.

b) Waiting for an extra half-hour while rehearsal runs over.

c) Fund raisers for trips that they don't feel are necessary.

d) Summer band camp that conflicts with family vacation.

e) Disciplinary action that is directed towards their son or daughter (of course, it's O.K. to use it on other students).

f) Criteria that are set for everything from majorettes to band officers (particularly if their son or daughter doesn't qualify).

g) Beating or maiming bandsmen during rehearsal; or guru techniques that destroy teen-age minds.

h) Etc.

Accept this fact about band parents; deal with it on a first-hand basis, and above all, be fair and honest. You can afford to lose a few battles in return for winning the war. They don't possess the expertise that you do, and furthermore, they don't care to. Band is an opportunity for their son or daughter to "shine," not you. If you keep this in mind at your next booster meeting, the forward progress will astound you—and keep smiling.

4. If there is one thing that we all have in common, it is the fact that we are selfish for the success of our programs. Nobody likes to be second best. We may accept it, but we know all the reasons why, and that is enough reason to keep trying. Keeping this in mind, never expect your colleagues to evaluate your band as you think it should be. Winning is a precious, but often lonely reward. If you have a super band, you can enjoy the prestige of being top dog, but realize that you are always a target for jealous comments. It's hard to understand that this is really an inverted form of envy. Too often, we try to defend our position, or put-down the other guy. This is really a shallow ego-builder. If you really are the best, tell no one. You won't have to—they'll know. Never take on one of your colleagues. If he is that important, keep him as a friend and share your knowledge with him. He obviously knows something

that you don't and you had better find out if you really want to be the best. Modesty represents a rare trait in our business. Give it a whirl—you'd be surprised how refreshing it can be. And all the time you are experimenting with it—keep smiling.

5. Not many spouses bargain for an entire band program as part of the marriage agreement. Sitting on a school bus for eight hours while hemming band trousers is not high on the list of romantic drives in today's fashion magazines. Being responsible for a cookout for 141 victorious band members is really quite more than having a few friends over. Serving dinner at the regular time of somewhere between 5:00 to 11:30 does not lend itself to the gourmet chef. Spending Friday night in the cold rain and trying to act excited about 200 people tramping around in the mud is not really the way to start off the weekend being together. Do you think that she realized this when she said, "for better or worse?" You can't change the job, but you can be sincerely appreciative of all that she gives you and all that she gives up for you. When you finally do fall through the front door in an exhausted last effort, save enough for a kiss and pleasant "I'm home." Let her know that you couldn't succeed without her—and the truth is, you probably couldn't. She should get more smiles than anybody. The list is endless, and if it has provoked any thought on your part, then my mission has been accomplished. You see, as well-trained as we are when we graduate from all our academic training, we really have no idea what we are expected to do. I clearly remember falling in my office chair one evening; it had been one of those days when everything that I did was in the wrong key. I had taken on a coach, my boss, a couple of parents, and a group of hostile band members. Just as I was about to fly the coop, my boss walked in and looked at me with a challenging sneer. I shook my head in defeat and whimpered, "You know, all I ever wanted to be was a band director, and I haven't heard one note of music today." His sneer turned to a warm smile and he put his arm around me and explained, "You are a band director, and a darned good one, and as soon as you realize that what you are doing is band-directing, you'll be a heck of a lot better!" You know, he was right; and do you know what else? It even made me smile.

*"Ideas are funny things—they don't work unless you do."*

# Silence is Golden:
# Playing Rests

It sounds silly, doesn't it? One doesn't *play* rests, one *rests* during rests. It would be more appropriate to say: one doesn't play one's instrument during the rests, but one does not take a mental vacation either. It is a matter of semantics for the most part, and certainly something few of us address in our rehearsals, let alone performances. Consider your own rehearsals whether it is concert band, jazz band, even marching band: do you not find all of the discipline problems and annoyances happening when the individual or the section is musically tacet and behaviorally double forte? How many times have we all used these familiar quotes: "Flutes, will you not whisper during the oboe solo!"; "Why are the third clarinets passing notes? Pay attention to me!"; "O.K., which saxophone is responsible for this paper airplane? It has to be in the tenors, because the altos were playing...anyway the fuselage is made from a chipped tenor reed!"; "French horns, who gave you permission to write letters during the second movement?"; "Trumpets, if you would not talk during the rests, you would know when to come in? And quit trading mouthpieces and tuning slides?"; "That's it, trombones! Either you quit squirting each other with the water bottles or we

go back to everybody playing in one position like the old days?";
"Baritones: you are supposed to be counting rests, not playing the
first trumpet part by ear"; "All right tubas, if I see any more food
back there, I'm going to make you go back to shop auto repair
class!"; "Drummers . . . sorry—*percussionists*: why is there a
puppy in the equipment cabinet? Who's going to clean up this
mess?"

Although we may be amused at these all too familiar statements, we know this is the very reason rehearsals bog down. By
the time we recover from recognizing one of these incongruent
behaviors, it has cost untold amounts of time, not to mention the
complete destruction of any musical mood created up to that point.
As a percussionist, I have many personal experiences of sitting/
standing through countless rehearsals without ever playing one
note. The temptation to create some kind of outside interest was
always dominant in my thinking—and, more than likely, manifested
somewhere along the line. Results: a tongue lashing from the
conductor (often deserved), and a halt to the forward progress of
the entire group. Not to mention the personal agony suffered by
the person behind the baton. Think back to your times of guest-
conducting and doing visitation clinics for your colleagues. Did
you spend all of your time working on intonation, phrasing,
balance, accidentals, or was some of it spent on deportment,
musical attitude, artistic conduct? Did any of your pleasantness
turn into aggravation? Were you tempted to stop the whole
rehearsal and express your thoughts about simple manners and
common decency? If you didn't respond yes to at least one of
these, many of us are interested in trading places with you.
Certainly this extraneous behavior is not generated to agitate the
director of the organization—at least in most cases. However, it
comes from lack of knowing what to do during those 126 measure
tacets.

Few teachers told us anything about playing rests other than,
"You're not supposed to be playing at letter B! Why are you
playing? Can't you count? The musician must understand that
everything they do during the rehearsal or performance is part of
the finished artistic product. One cannot escape or disappear, but
must realize how he or she fits into the holistic spectrum and
weave of the final product. In other words: Get with the program!
The responsibility of the musician goes well beyond playing the
right notes. Visual messages to the brain have a greater impact
than audio messages, assuming they both have the same intensity

level. Therefore, the beauty of a legato clarinet passage will be destroyed by a trumpet player falling off the back of the risers, or a drummer signaling his girlfriend in the alto sax section, or a flute player fluffing the back of her hair. It's doubtful that any of these acts are a purposeful sabotage of the clarinets' moment in the spotlight, but that is precisely the results. It serves as a diversion to everyone, even the clarinet section. How often have we attended or conducted the elementary band's first concert and observed students waving to Mom, Dad, Grandma, Grandpa, whomever? The point is, we need to be spending time talking about how to play rests. Part of being an all-around musician is the understanding of this important facet of performance. There are certain accepted behaviors, and to violate these standards/ disciplines is just as costly to the group as playing the wrong notes. When the proper rest technique is not part of the curriculum, you can expect to witness a new form of creativity. Those rests will get played, somehow or another. Wouldn't you like to have some artistic direction on *how* they get played? Most of our rehearsal time is spent working on details in the technical realm of the various instruments, and after all, that is our job: *to teach music*. We simply need to take into account that part of music is silence— rests. The attention to this particular detail will offer the conductor a fresh new approach to rehearsals and will, in fact, improve the rehearsals for everyone involved; not to mention the overall on-stage (or on-field) performance. The time gained through the focus of energy is remarkable, and the sense of pride instilled via the importance of each individual, even during the rests, gives a new meaning and direction to the entire ensemble—even to the percussionist who must count 256 measures for one triangle note. We all have been well-trained at teaching notes, let us now explore the exciting world of teaching rests. Silence is golden.

*"Keep your mind open;*
*something good might enter."*

# Caution: Band Directing
# May Be Hazardous
# To Your Health!

"I'm tired, I'm out of new ideas, I'm frustrated, I'm underpaid and over-worked, nobody understands my situation, I've had it with parents trying to make my decisions, my personal life is a wreck, the students don't really care, there's no future in this job, we'll never get the performance ready on time, I've lost my keys, my own children don't recognize me, my office looks like a garbage dump from McDonald's, Burger King, and Wendy's, my shoes have holes in the soles, I have a hole in my soul, seven uniforms cannot be accounted for, the budget is overspent by $6,000, the percussion instructor ran off with the drum major who was also my all-state oboist, our Christmas Concert is scheduled on the same night as the Community Concert Series with Michael Jackson, and I haven't been to a dentist in four years. And all I wanted to be was a band director."

"I'm burned out!"

## BAND DIRECTOR BURN-OUT (BDBO)

A common affliction that can strike at any time without warning. The symptoms are easily identifiable: exhaustion, overwhelm, anxiety, stomach upset, confusion, depression, disorganization, anger, hostility, fear, an administration that can't seem to hear, students who don't seem to care, and a 1977 Plymouth with bad head gaskets—but still runs!

The prescription for this disease is often suggested by other directors—your friends—with the same disease; and it goes something like this:

More coffee, more cigarettes, lock yourself in the office, gripe, get upset and blame your students, host your own "Pity Party," throw a tantrum in front of everyone to certify your insanity!, more junk food, no exercise or fresh air, lots of TV, avoidance of any responsibility, and absolutely no communication with anyone.

There you have it. Now, you can boast of a severe case of BDBO (Band Director Burn-out). You may even be a candidate for the next "Band Director Who Got Dumped On The Most of the Year Award" at the next state convention. You'll have to really, really be burned out because a lot of people are after this award.

One of the worst things about this illness concerns the fact that the people who have it will defend their ailment. They will take every last bit of energy to explain why they have no energy—and we laugh at dogs who chase their tails. Yet we will support humans who chase their tails.

We have come to accept this non-curable plague of burn-out as a reality, and this label is becoming a reason to leave a profession which was chosen because of a desire to share a gift with young people so they could experience some of the tremendous rewards only the art of music can offer. There is such a paradox in all of this, much like pushing and pulling with the same pair of hands and then wondering why we aren't going anywhere!

Before any defenses create a wall of non-communication, let's admit the realities of the profession: anxiety, long hours, lack of appreciation, Murphy's Law, disappointment in excess, deadlines, and on, and on. This is part of it, and also part of the challenge of surviving it. If you aren't willing to deal with these realities, then, for certain, you have chosen the wrong profession and you are a likely victim of BDBO—in fact, it is predictable, much like a person who says, "I want to be a surgeon, but I can't stand the sight of blood.

I'm convinced that if being a band director meant a life of directing the band, we would have: 1. A lot more people choosing to be band directors. 2. Many more people staying in the profession. Sometimes it seems the least amount of a band director's time is spent on the podium. Other things seem to get in the way: testing, picture-taking, fund-raising, parent-meetings, trip plans, announcements, teacher strikes, figuring out how to use the new computer, etc.

With all of this data available, we should be able to come up with a good antidote for BDBO, and it is not another solution to these various problems, but an overall attitude about the problems and an approach to solving them which will add to our excitement and momentum rather than drain our energy supply. Consider this information about the way we live:

Our Western philosophy is geared towards asking "Why did this happen to me?" at the onset of any set of circumstances. "Why did my 1st chair trumpet move to a neighboring school district? Why did we miss a 1st division by only one point? Why did our buses break down on the way to the festival? Why did the football team have to make it to the State finals so we're still marching in December?" In other words, we immediately assume an emotional posture which sends all of our thinking through a defensive mental filter. And we all know that the defense rarely scores any points.

Contrary to this, the Eastern philosophy tends to ask this question: "What is there for me to learn from this situation and use to my benefit?" So rather than a reaction basis of understanding, we have taken on a positive action form of reasoning: "Since my 1st chair trumpet has moved, it will give me the chance to see which member of the section is ready to meet this challenge. What a great opportunity there is for all of them to grow in this situation. The entire section has the chance to improve and develop. Since we're only 1 point away from a 1st division, and we played well, the students can reach a new level of musical and technical proficiency. This can really be a great incentive to go for it and better our entire band. Since we have one bus not running, we can all gather on the other two buses and make it to the festival while learning a new kind of cooperation and group effort—a new test of our we-us family attitude. The success of the football team will afford us the chance to perform for several more thousand people as well as stretch our resources to see if we can prepare our

Christmas Concert at the same time; a chance to make the most of a great opportunity and learn time management at the same time for the future."

Easier said than done. Not really, because you will survive the situation. You always do, you must have survived, otherwise you wouldn't be reading this. With that information available, why not tackle the problem offensively and score some points along the way? The alternative approach—upset, frustration, why me?—is certain to cause you, not to mention your students, anguish, nervous tension, and contribute a huge chunk to your Burn-Out Band, plus the always-present temptation to cash it all in.

It really is a very simply choice we all make every moment of our lives: "Will I let the circumstances control my attitude and actions, or my attitude and actions control my circumstances?" It is unbelievable that people will choose the path of personal discomfort—self-abuse—which is the one common factor in all band director burn-out cases.

So what's the solution? How does one avoid this dilemma? Is BDBO terminal? Is there hope? BDBO is a result of a thought-process. We reason ourselves into the disease. Once the victim accepts the affliction, all future thinking and choice-making is based on "I know I'm just burned-out." Therefore, every new set of circumstances is controlled by this reasoning which confirms the original prognosis; which strengthens the belief of the disease, reconfirming the thought and choice-making process—a no-win race. Before long, the filter is so dominant, we begin to behave accordingly and identify the problem (BDBO) and this further reinforces the belief. The agreement factor comes into play and now we must live-up to our weakness; since we're burned-out we must behave in that role. And, as we all know, soon the role begins to control the action. And, sure enough, we become burned out.

At this stage of the game, the way out is twofold:

1. Quit. Change your circumstances. But beware: you must be very careful or you'll carry the ailment with you into your next profession if you continue to let your circumstances control your attitude.

2. Change your thought process. Ultimately, this is what you will have to do even if you choose option 1: the people who leave the profession and seem to find instant happiness have simply changed their thought process in the transition. In other words, they have chosen to be excited about their work.

The human being is brilliant and possesses unlimited potential, yet we are still creatures of habit. Our mental approach to anything is a learned habit. Approaching each moment positively isn't something that just happens. It must be practiced, refined, practiced more, and at times, almost demanded. Each time you avoid reaction and seek positive action, you not only handle the present situation with greater personal security, but you strengthen your own thought-process and assume a greater benefit package for the next set of circumstances. Know that this same formula applies to a negative approach: we behave according to the habits we set. Positive habits produce positive behavior; negative habits produce negative behavior.

BDBO is a result of negative thinking. Sometimes it also seems to be a generic reason to leave the profession, when, in reality the person simply wants to change jobs for a host of other reasons: More revenue, fewer hours, relocation, family, etc. We seem to need to justify our choice to give it up, and BDBO is always a good catch-all reason which is seldom challenged. Sympathy and understanding run high among colleagues in the profession since we all have had the disease in one form or another.

If you feel as though you are burning-out and still want to be a band director, read the following books by Dr. Wayne Dyer before you make any decisions in a state of emotional or physical unrest. Yes, even though you don't have the time to read them, it will be worth your while:

1. *Your Erroneous Zones.* A great introduction to self-help learning. Bold and to the point.

2. *Pulling Your Own Strings.* An excellent chance to see what is possible in our lives; thrilling.

3. *The Sky's The Limit.* Exciting, motivating, and quite tender.

4. *Gifts from Eykis.* Brilliant, a must if you expect to survive this life being happy.

From here on you will find many more wonderful authors. Seek them out! Don't miss the opportunity to read all of Dr. Leo Buscaglia's works: an outstanding modern-way philosopher.

One last bit of information. We all hear the horror stories of how the band world is being destroyed by academic requirement-revisions, teacher cutbacks, economic crises, noncommittal attitudes of today's students, etc. These circumstances do exist and serve as fear motivators to acquire BDBO, but they are certainly not destroying our band programs. In many cases, they have brought people together to save the band, and as a result have strengthened the band. As I travel from coast-to-coast working with bands in every part of the country, I find:

1. Parents who are extremely interested and willing to lend their support; they want the best for their children.

2. Communities who are totally behind the band program—in both financial support and spirit.

3. An incredibly high level of commitment from the students; discipline and excellence always produce quality.

4. Band directors who are going above and beyond the call of duty in every facet of their work; setting new levels of achievement and breaking new ground.

5. An exciting momentum in our future direction. We are growing.

You do make a positive difference for so many. Our profession needs qualified and dedicated teachers who can share their talents and offer leadership in teaching excellence through music. You can make an impact. You don't have time to get burned out.

Wisely stated by one of our greatest philosophers: "Success is getting what you want; happiness is wanting what you get."

*"When you make your mark on the world,
watch out for the guys with erasers."*

# Success Products
# for Band Directors

There is absolutely no question that our music industry
has done an outstanding job in supplying us with everything we
could possibly need to become effective band directors. From
specially designed semi-trailers for our equipment, right down to
the mini-metronome-tuner for that final check just prior to down-
beat. There are even computers to write our marching band shows
and color video recorders and players which afford us a review/
correction opportunity never before available in our profession.
What more could we ask for? We have it all.

Well, not quite. There are a few areas where our marketing
friends have failed, and it is high time we addressed these areas of
need. We owe it to ourselves and our industry compatriots to bring
this void to their attention. Should any of you reading this article
choose to produce these items, you can rest assured you will have
an eager customer list awaiting the chance to purchase any or all
of these immediately.

**Band Products for the Future**

1. PERMA-SUB. This would be a robot-like character which
could substitute for any missing member of the band. Special
adapters would fit on the creature's mouth so it would be flexible
in terms of instrumentation. Utilizing a computer-brain, PERMA-

SUB could be programmed via floppy disks to sit in wherever a member of the band was missing due to illness, testing, track meets, or a McDonald's run. Included in the initial purchase price would be three standard micro-programs: Felicia-the Flirting Flutist, Clyde-the Clever Clarinetist, and Tommy-the Tooting Trumpet. Additional programs are available at a nominal fee: Sarah-a Saxophone Symphony, Olga-the Erroneous Oboe, Fanny-the French Horn Phenomenon, and Lars-the Low Brass Legend. Percussion disks are not sold: simply turn the machine loose without any sense of direction.

2. PRINCIPAL PAL. Similar in design to PERMA-SUB, this product is designed to serve as an administrator who cooperates and understands how band directors operate. Along with PRINCI-PAL PAL comes an unlimited budget, a complete curriculum including 5 free preparatory periods per day, an annual 32% salary increase, and three trial lawyers. PRINCIPAL PAL can be neatly tucked away in the back of one's desk and never used if you hate administrator communication. PRINCIPAL PAL never writes notes, has no interest in trophies, feels that music should be the first consideration in the scheduling process, and can keep time. PRINCIPAL PAL needs no upkeep or personal attention and feels that purchase orders are a waste of time. For an additional $2,400 you can purchase the deluxe version: POWERFUL PRINCIPAL PAL. This model has three children enrolled in the band who think you are a fantastic teacher.

3. PERFORMANCE UTOPIA PREPARATION EXERCISES (PUPE). This collection of fundamental exercises includes scales, lip slurs, excerpts, and traditional excuses for not playing the part, and is organized in such a manner that the student does not have to spend any time practicing the material. He or she simply places the book beneath a pillow at night, and the information is transmitted via cosmic imagery into their brains. SUPER PUPE, an advanced version of PUPE, is available for those who wish to become all-state players but cannot practice their music due to drama club auditions or Senior Prom committees.

4. BOOSTER BONANZA. Certain to be one of the most popular of the product line, BOOSTER BONANZA brings to your program an unlimited supply of revenue, financial ties to every facet of your community, and a free demonstrator car from your local Ford dealer. As a part of this package you will receive a U.S. Senator, a local real estate tycoon who was a former trombonist, and a wealthy travel agent who insists you take

orientation trips to Hawaii every six weeks. And for just a few dollars more, you can purchase BOLD BOOSTER BONANZA featuring a bonus character known as Alfredo "Hit-Man" Fettucini, a personal side-kick who will be with you at all times to insure smooth sailing in working with others.

5. HAPPY HOME. Is there any doubt this will be the first of the new products on every band director's budget request? HAPPY HOME comes complete with: house, two-car garage (one side to be used for band props), miniature football field in the back, two talented teenagers (bassoonist who can double on viola and a screech jazz trumpeter who does arrangements which can be sold to colleagues), and a SPOUSE who directs the church choir, plays piano accompaniments, and is on the Board of Directors of Apple Computer, Inc. HAPPY HOME is designed so there can be no fighting while in the environment, but everyone must be dedicated to the welfare of YOU and the growth and development of the band.

And last but certainly not least:

6. VICTORY VANITY. Although the cost of this catalogue item far exceeds anything else available, it is a must for the aspiring young director who wants it all. VICTORY VANITY is multi-faceted and can be used with concert band, jazz band, marching band, and even small ensembles. (Color guard versions are available, but need the jealously retainer added to the original format.) VICTORY VANITY will insure first place at each and every contest and festival. If you are interested in the SWEEP-STAKES option, it requires you relinquish product #5: HAPPY HOME. VICTORY VANITY is guaranteed to fill your rehearsal room with trophies, plaques, and countless letters of commendation. It is suggested you buy the maintenance contract with this product. It is called EGO ERASER—An absolute necessity.

So, if you want to be at the leading edge of this profession, it is time to start saving for these new and exciting items of support. However, if your budget does not allow you to consider this kind of luxurious extravagance, may we suggest you go about accomplishing all of this on your own. You can, you know. Heed the wise old saying: "If you want it done right, do it yourself."

*"All our resolves and decisions are made in a
mood or frame of mind which is certain to change!"*
—Marcel Proust

# Bounce Back with the Basketball Band

Let's discuss something that many of you don't like to think about: basketball band. No big deal, right? Just tack up a "volunteer sign-up sheet," twist the arms of a few of the lead players, substitute your jazz band and set drummer for the marching drum section, pass out the "Top 40 Easy Arrangement" booklets and you're ready to roll. Rah Rah, sis-boom bah, "GO-FIGHT-TIGERS," and you're off on another Roaring-Boring season of gymnasium hysteria. There are many of you who have seen the opportunity to embellish your existing program and offer non-band students exciting reasons to get on the bandwagon. Bravo!

Then there are those of you who resist this performance group with such determinism that in spite of many talented players, it still doesn't achieve its purpose, let alone build additional strength into the band program. This article is directed to those of you who: (1) don't like to deal with the basketball band; (2) have not had measurable success with pep bands; (3) would like to change the present image of your basketball band; (4) want to find the solution to this thorn in your side; and (5) (last—but perhaps the most important of all) are out there to do the best job you possibly can in every aspect of your work, and know that if there is more to learn and new movements on the horizon, you want to be in on the ground floor. Basketball arrives at the worst possible time of the year—immediately after marching season when everyone is tired, and just prior to the big concert-festival marathon. So what's the solution? How do you reach down into that magic, musical top hat and pull out another winner? How do you coax all the band to continue an exhausting rehearsal schedule? How can you justify to your administration, your students, your colleagues, your band parents, your family, and most of all, to yourself, any educational worth that balances the necessary investment ahead? The first step takes no time at all: simply choose if you really do want an excellent basketball band and if you are willing to assume the responsibility for its creation and growth. If your answer is no, read no further: stop. However, if your answer is "Yes, maybe . . . I think so . . . could be . . . show me how," or any number of other curious, but not-so-certain answers, then today just might be your lucky day; you may go home tonight a little more excited and a lot more on target about what basketball games can mean to your band program. To begin with, you must see basketball games in the same light that you do football games. These people—the fans—need to be entertained and the spotlight is on whoever takes advantage of the exposure possibilities. Right before your very eyes, you have a captive audience; you didn't even have to do the publicity. If you don't put something out for them to watch, somebody else will—it's your option at this point: go for it!

Now, let's be sane: in football you are responsible to several thousand people, so you give them twirlers, rifles, drill teams, tall flags, swing flags, percussion features, lots of horns, dance steps, soloists, streamers, and a host of other three-ring circus devices to assure crowd reaction and maintain the "our band's the greatest in the land" attitude.

If a basketball crowd is one-fourth as large as a football crowd, use that as a measure in planning your basketball halftime activities. By being inside a gymnasium, several options are available that cannot be effectively used outside: recorded music, amplification for soloists, closer contact with the crowd for special spotlights, placement of players for antiphonal effects, more detail to facial expression and body movement subtleties, not to mention the more focused center of attention and the built-in sound shell.

The obvious groups to begin with in dressing up your basketball half-times are the various auxiliary corps of the marching band. It's not unusual for these units to spend much of the summer and all of the fall season perfecting a skill which is put on the shelf once the marching band has completed the last half-time show. If these people are not converts (a person choosing to be in an auxiliary unit during marching season but returns to playing a band instrument during the remainder of the year), they tend to drift into the student body never to be seen again, or they are constantly clamoring at your office door in search of an outlet for their talent. Too often, this is met with the predictable pacifier that spring auditions are not far away. This is a perfect opportunity to support your program and kill several birds with one stone.

1. Each auxiliary group can plan a 4 to 5 minute routine to present as a basketball halftime feature using recorded music so that it does not require extra band rehearsal.

2. It affords these people the chance to improve their skills and exposes them in a feature presentation where they are the stars of the show.

3. The recruiting potential is increased as it becomes very fashionable to be a part of this respected performing group.

4. The band program gets another community vote of approval due to the obvious concern and dedication to the fans in providing top quality entertainment.

5. The band members observe the performance and add their endorsement since they also share in the compliments to follow.

The positive-support possibilities are endless, and the entire concept brings maximum benefits for the investment. One of the greatest sources of creativity for entertainment is growing in your own backyard, and here is a chance to use it: it's your own band members and their wealth of individual talents combined with their energetic up-to-date familiarity with what's happening. It could be everything from unicycle demonstration to a Frisbee contest. Their unrestricted imaginations will create entertainment possibilities that you never before considered. These, combined with your openness and knowledge of presentation, and the support of the band providing the music (or participating in some fashion) spells success any way you look at it.

The excitement that is generated by the marching band does not have to dwindle during the basketball season. In fact, use that momentum to your advantage: keep the ball rolling (no pun intended) and allow the community to see that their vital financial and vocal support is appreciated and counted on during the entire year and that the band program is eager to show off all that has been contributed in good faith. Keep that attitude of performance high in the minds of the bandsmen and let them share in the rewards that come with it. Allow yourself the pleasure of letting go. And afford the program the opportunity to expand and breathe. Be brave. Refresh your band members, your community, and most of all yourself. Be clever, be tasteful, be innovative...be you! It's a shame not to go for it!

*"Where I was is destroyed, where I
am stands condemned, where I shall
be is just now being built."*

# The Most
# Important Audience

Mom and Dad are still the most important audience.
Ask any young musicians who they want to hear them play, sing,
march, etc., and they will tell you, "My parents."

Although we are living in a day and age where the family unit
is struggling against divorce, economic strains, change in social
standards, and a heavy emphasis on the I-me concept of living,
there is still a basic desire to please Mother and Father. When a
young person spends countless hours in preparation for a performance, and a parent is not on hand to support and acknowledge
this accomplishment, then something is incomplete for the student.

Granted, parents have all kinds of extra duties to handle and
time is certainly at a premium. It is easy to rationalize: missing a
booster meeting, promising to make the next concert, pleading too
tired for any more responsibilities. We can always find excuses for
not going the extra mile, and sure, there will be future booster
meetings, and certainly other concerts to attend—and, perhaps,
there will be a surge of energy when we will look forward to extra
responsibilities. Dream on.

As music educators, our job is to teach music; maybe, just

maybe, we should also think about educating parents in terms of the worth of being involved relative to their son or daughter's musical life. Heaven forbid, we would tell them how to be better parents. Rather we might suggest the many benefits to them and to the relationship with their child via this kind of supportive participation. Since Mom and Dad are the most important audience, there is much to be gained when they are on hand to witness this musical accomplishment, not to mention what might be lost when they are absent.

When parents are present at a concert it says:
1. They care about me.
2. They support me in my musical growth.
3. They think it is important I go the distance.
4. They want to see me attain excellence.
5. The priorities in my life are important to them.
6. I'm worth their time, even though they have other choices.
7. They think my efforts are worthy—and I'm worthy.
8. They recognize my dedication and encourage my learning.
9. They know being there means a lot to me.
10. My performance and their attendance is an expression of our love for one another.

It seems that so many parents think they are just coming to a concert when, in reality, they are attending a performance of their child. We have all seen Mom and Dad give standing ovations to musical performances which left much to be desired. They were not acknowledging the music, they were expressing their heartfelt pride in the effort put forth by their child. The worth of this action in regards to the self esteem of the performers is immeasurable. It means: "All my efforts, all my sacrifice, all my learning was worthwhile. I made a difference—I count." Needless to say, the impetus to do even better is planted securely in the mind. And the mind leads itself in the direction of its most dominant thought.

Certainly there is much internal satisfaction which comes from a fine musical performance; however, this may be reserved for a chosen few during those first few years of learning, practicing, and rehearsing while others are outside playing. Young musicians need all the support we can muster or the options for a less difficult activity may become more attractive. This is certainly a time in growing when they need us (parents, teachers) the most in helping to focus the energy.

Parent approval is the most potent fuel when it comes to insuring success for any young person. Yes, we all want the parents to appreciate and understand Mozart, Handel, Wagner, Holst, etc. And, certainly that will come with time, just as it did for us. But it is necessary for them to appreciate and understand what it means to their son and daughter to have Mom and Dad in the audience.

If we can get them to attend just one performance, much of this mission is accomplished. The energy generated via child and parent during a performance is addictive. It creates a feeling beyond words and brings the whole event to a new level. What parents would not want to be part of such an incredible experience?

Yes, there will always be those who never make the effort, but let us make sure we have combed the ranks to seek out all those who are unaware of what an important role they play in the musical growth of their child. Perhaps we will never get 100%, but we should not be satisfied until we've tried every trick in the book, and created a few of our own. Rather than explain why many parents aren't attending, let's put our efforts on getting them there.

After hearing countless excuses and questioning yourself "Is this really all worthwhile," just keep remembering: for the students, Mom and Dad are still the most important audience in the world.

*"One reason that big apples are
always on the top of the basket is
that there are always a lot of little
ones holding them up there."*

# Why Do We Do It?

W hy do we do it? Why do we insist on going outside
during the hottest time of the year and strap on drums which cause
excruciating pain to the collar bone, try to keep horns to our mouth
in some sort of workable embouchure, (yes, even with braces
cutting into our inner lips), and throwing flags, rifles, batons and
all other kinds of make-shift guard substitutes over the tops of
each other? If successful, nobody gets hurt; if not, get the
bandages out and try again. We spend countless hours charging up
and down the rehearsal field, learning, relearning, reworking,
refining, until we simply run out of time and are faced squarely
with a performance deadline. What's the payoff for all this effort?
Only a person deeply involved in the activity could even begin
to understand the answer to this perplexing question. Only someone
who has ignored the parched throat and unbearable thirst so there
could be one more run-through knows the answer. Only the
directors and staff, who press beyond much needed sleep so they
can rewrite for the next day's practice, know the answer. Only the
parents who drive countless miles, readjust their family schedules
and sell every product under the sun to raise the support funds
know the answer. Everyone who has touched the activity, in any
way, from bus driver to fan in the stands has the fever. It is an

extraordinary phenomena which says, "I want to be the best I can be—to push myself to the ultimate limit and to share this journey with others who feel the same!"

Few people ever know what it is to devote 100 percent of their energy to one goal. We are a society which skims off the top. Our basic needs are met and most of our life is seeking a higher level of luxury in hopes it will bring with it a greater sense of peace and fulfillment. Of course, real happiness comes from giving and when we combine a group of people all possessing musical talent, the process of putting together a quality production offers a challenge that no real champion can refuse. The inner feeling of satisfaction cannot be measured in worldly terms. A great performance cannot be compared to a new stereo, or a sports car. It is a personal understanding which makes everything else secondary to the value of knowing we did it.

Therein lies the answer to the question: Why do we do it? There is an unquenchable desire in the human being to break through to new levels. Even when we accomplish something of significant acclaim there will certainly be a challenge to do it faster, more flawlessly and more creatively. We simply won't allow status quo to prevail, whether it be in the field of medicine, where it is now commonplace to replace worn out organs, or sports, where the once impossible four minute mile is being run by high school students, or yes, even the marching activity where we are now enjoying field performances by teenagers which would have been scoffed at as totally impossible in 1950. We see the limits are flexible. That basic need to contribute something to humanity serves as an indescribable motivational force which we all share.

Knowing this is fundamental in performing, teaching or even observing. The sense of appreciation comes from the effort, not the results. It is the planning, practicing, organizing sharing, day-by-day putting it together which is the pay-off. Certainly not the trophy, or score, or medallion. The feeling of self-worth cannot be transferred to a plastic trophy, nor can a trophy by itself insure the feeling of self-worth. It is that down-deep, within yourself, bottom of the gut realization: "That's my ultimate effort so far--a new level which will serve as a stepping stone to an even higher level."

I once had a student who had been injured in a car accident during childhood and his leg was severely handicapped. He was a fine trumpet player and could hold his own musically with anyone in the organization. Of course, marching band proved a different story. For two years, he sidelined and watched his friends enjoy the many benefits of the challenge. The third year, he chose to march. We all watched as he struggled with every step having to use three times as much energy as everyone else just to keep up. Many hours following rehearsal were spent in a whirlpool easing the muscle pain of the bad leg. During the breaks, band members would bring water to him so he would not have to walk across the field to the water cooler. Needless to say, he became a role model for all of us. Most people would have thrown in the towel, but his desire to break through to a new level was dominant; there was not a chance he was going to quit. Certainly one of the greatest victories for the band centers on this young man's field performance. As he marched proudly, with a slight limp, to his opening position in the show, everyone could sense he was about to lead all of us to a new level. The performance was extraordinary, and as each second passed, the momentum of the band grew. The sound was filled with strength and emotion and the execution of every move was filled with exploding energy. It was as if the music and the marching came together as one. The guard work became the music and the blend of countless hours of hard work seemed to all melt into the band's expression of giving. The young trumpet player with the bad leg could not be identified from anyone else as the noticeable limp was no longer evident. Whatever the price we had to pay for this moment in time, it was worth it many times over. Why we do it became vividly clear: we do it to give and to share our basic desire for excellence with one another. Every person involved in the activity has a similar story, and all of these experiences confirm and serve as a testimony to the unbelievable benefits which are available to all of us by giving 100 percent.

Perhaps this book will not make the lines any straighter, or the spacing any better, or the blend any richer, but it may remind us what a privilege it is to be a part of an environment where we are encouraged to seek new heights, to reach beyond the known limits, to seek quality in everything we do. If so, then there is no doubt, the lines will be straighter, spacing better, and the blend will evidence our efforts to continue to grow and learn. When asked why he wanted to climb Mt. Everest, the explorer commented, "Because it's there." Do you see some of yourself in that explorer? To meet the obstacles and break through them, so we can meet more obstacles to break through, etc. It's the opportunity of a lifetime. And for many of us, it is a lifetime. March on.

*"Each man has many faces: those he
exhibits, those he has, those he thinks he has,
and those he hopes he will one day have."*

# Just One More
# For the Road

How many days left? The countdown is on and the
anticipation of the summer vacation is almost more than walls of
the school can contain. Teachers are thinking of excuses to hold
class outside and students are thinking about everything but
classes. Not the band director, though. No—here is the teacher of
teachers who started prior to regular school with pre-school
marching band camp, and will be the last to leave putting away
equipment and music from the Commencement Band. (Let us not
forget the 4th of July parade and the summer concert in the park
duties.)

Do you go through all of those post-school questions which
make it seem like nothing was accomplished during the entire
year? Are you absolutely oblivious to the activities which surrounded you everyday? Here is a typical scene as our most
successful generic band director takes the last stroll through the
band facilities as the final chord of "Procession of the Nobles" still
rings in the deserted gymnasium.

We just bought 140 new uniforms this year and I can only
account for 111 in the storage room. You don't suppose the

Seniors decided to keep their uniform as a souvenir?

• I know when I passed out "America the Beautiful" all the sax parts were there; now why is there no saxophone music and all the sax folders have tuba music and tearouts from field and stream? No wonder it sounded so bad.

• Speaking of tubas, what is this in Clarence Clunker's tuba bell? For heaven sakes, it's Jerry Jocko's gym clothes. I remember him putting up a sigh about his missing athletic wear back in mid-February. You don't suppose this has been in the tuba since then? Wait—I've got hold of it—there! Well no doubt the clothes have been there since February. Make a note to inform Jerry his athletic apparel is outside the band hall.

• Now what's this box of stuff back here in the percussion section? Oh no! We just bought those maracas! Well, at least they tried to tape the little beads back in. Here's Greg Shotput's Chemistry text. Seems like he told me he was flunking chemistry; no wonder, the book has never been opened except to put his name on the inside cover. Yep, Greg spelled his name wrong again. No problem, he has a full scholarship to play football at the local college.

• Let's check the storage room for the auxiliary groups. This should be a matter of just looking in and seeing that everything is all-right since they are such winners. Why last year they won the state/national/international tall flag, pom, dance single twirl division. If I remember right, there were two other groups in their category—one didn't appear. The girls were so excited they took a week off school and went to Orlando as a reward for their efforts. Thirty-eight of them made the trip and thirty-four returned. Some stayed to dance in the latest Disney production. I know it upset the parents, but kids will be kids. Oh dear, this room looks like a cyclone hit it. Aren't these the state-of-the-art flags we bought last fall for $82.75 each? What are they doing rolled up under the wheels of the bass amp? The bass amp! I found the bass amp! That means Stan Slyface was expelled for no reason at all. I was afraid to tell anyone we lost the bass amp. How do you suppose it got back in here? I'll just flip it on to make sure it still works...wait a minute, somebody has taken all the insides out of it. My heavens, there aren't even any speakers left. Well, Stan got exactly what he deserved. Maybe I'll just close this room off and call the captains to come in and clean it up. Wait . . . I thought I heard something. I did! There's someone in here. "Hello. I'll get you out, just keep whimpering so I can find you." If I can just move this drum major's podium that Mr. Crafto donated to the band; his brother-in-law works at a marble quarry. Man, is this thing heavy! No wonder we didn't take it to the away games. There. My gosh, it's Missy Dollface. "Missy, I thought you were in Orlando with the other three girls! Good to have you back. Go get a quick drink of water and then come back and clean up this room!"

• Practice rooms; what could possibly be wrong in a practice room? Now this practice room looks more like an apartment than a practice room. Isn't this cute, they even have a little mailbox for messages. And here, all this time, I thought Mary and John were getting ready for solo-ensemble contest. They are such a special couple—nice decor for such a small room.

• Library—I have to take a look at the music library. This should be spit-polished. Priscilla Perfect spent most of the year reorganizing every piece of music and she never does anything wrong. Well, this is refreshing: a place for everything and everything in its place. Everyone loves Priscilla because she is the epitome of a perfect student. Let's see that everything is alphabetized. What's this? Priscilla would never read these kinds of magazines! Look in this file. My gosh, it's the grading key to this year's SAT tests! If I recall, Prissy did score in the upper 1% of the nation. Will you look at this—the guts to the bass amp with a "Paid in Full" receipt to Stan Slyface. What's this weird little gadget? It's one of those key-maker machines—and look at all the blank keys. And there's the master key I lost last October! Here's a mailing list for everyone in the school; and a "mail back card" packet with all their names and addresses on each one. $29.50 per master key plus postage and shipping. Wow! No wonder Priscilla has a new Mazda RX7. Where do you suppose she got all the paper to make those cards? Aha! That explains where all of our music has been going! I thought I remembered ordering *Pines of Rome*.

• What's left? Oh no! The instrument room. This is going to be the worst—I can't bear to look! Well, what a surprise: this room looks great! The shelves are clean and there are no instruments out of place. Wait. There are no instruments at all! What have they done with the instruments? Carl Certain promised to check in all the school horns after the graduation ceremonies. He even told me everything was taken care of. I just assumed that meant he had it all handled responsibly. Wait, here's a note: "Dear Friends, Thanks for all the great memories from our band family. Wish I could give each of you a thousand dollars for all the super times we shared, but I don't have that kind of money. So, just keep your horn as a token of my thanks—you've earned it! This will be especially neat for the seniors because you already have your uniforms as part of your band memorabilia. Thanks for you support. We're number #1! With all my love, Carl. P. S., If you want to sell your horn, call Priscilla P.; her boyfriend is a fence and can unload it in less than a day. Have a great summer!"

• The only place left is my office. This has been the most frightening experience of my life. It all looked like it was working so smoothly. This is the best year we ever had—and now to realize what disasters were right before my very eyes! I've got to be the worst band director in the nation. So what if we got Superior ratings at the playing contest? I really have failed as a teacher, a mentor of young people. These students are going to have to go out and face life and look at the deplorable job I have done in preparing them. Just let me sit here in my office and decide what is the best plan of action...I can't go on like this. There needs to be some accountability factor for the students—and for me.

What's this? Where did this package come from? Why look, it's a beautiful watch—and it's engraved on the back: "To Our Number 1 Teacher—Your Loving Staff 1986." What's the card say? "Dear Band Director, Don't worry about the uniforms and the horns. We have them safe and sound and will return them at band camp. Priscilla made copies of all the music before she did the mail-back cards and it is being put into new folders that Prissy brought with her key funds. Don't worry about the keys: she didn't make copies of the *real* master. The one you lost is in Jerry J's gym bag; check Clarence's tuba bell! Sly will be delivering a new bass amp to your house—it's lots nicer than the one the band now has. Oh—can you make it to Mary and John's wedding? Some of us will be playing for the ceremony—another reason we needed to have the horns this summer. Did you find Missy? Don't worry, she hadn't been there long! We thought you would be so glad to see her that you wouldn't care that she was stuffed behind the marble monster. Most of us Seniors will be at band camp to help with the new people; it's the least we can do for all that you have given to us. Have a restful vacation. We'll see you at band camp. With Love, Your Band Family." What a great card and letter. I knew they would never let me down. I love those kids. Kind of unusual stationary they used. Oh no, it's the back of the saxophone music to "America the Beautiful"! I wonder if they will remember there is a 4th of July parade and we will need the instruments, uniforms, and bass amp?! Yeah, they'll remember. I think the real reason they did it was so I would call and have them come back and march with the band at the parade. They are so special and have made my life so special. I'll make a few phone calls; they would probably like to have just one more for the road.

*"The measure of a man's real character
is what he would do if he knew he
would never be found out."*

# The Proverbial
# Summer Vacation!

At last—Summer! Freedom! A time all to myself. No more rehearsals, concerts, parades, booster meetings, faculty committees, etc.—just total rest and relaxation. Oh, how I have looked forward to getting away from it all. I don't even want to think about music for three months. This is going to be the most wonderful summer of my life; I've earned it and I am going to enjoy every second of doing exactly what I want to do.

Does that sound familiar? How about almost word for word in terms of your own thinking? Has somebody been inside your brain listening to you talk? Have you been thinking about those lazy, hazy, crazy days of summer?

Utopia, ecstasy, bliss, heaven—and all that jazz. There is no question that somewhere during our college education, some-one—probably through subversive hypnotic suggestion—led us to believe that summer would be a time for fun and frolic: you know, a chance to blow off the dust and clean out the cobwebs. They lied. Yet, even the veterans in this music education world continue to approach each summer with the fantasy running at full speed in their minds. Other teachers spend the summer gardening, vacationing, remodeling their house, spending time with the family, camping, sharing lemonade with Aunt Rhoda, and having three hour luncheons just prior to the afternoon golf game. Not true if you live in the world of music. Let's take a look at Mr. or Mrs. Successful Band Director and see what summer vacation has in store for him or her.

With a little creative imagination, we can crawl inside their minds and catch the reasoning process in action. Observe carefully as we eavesdrop on our friend's ego chattering wildly (as always) in preparation for the summer vacation ahead.

"O.K, you only have 6 more days to go and you're out of here. That's gonna be great! All the concerts are finished, festival is completed, no more performances: this is gonna be terrific. All that's left to do is the graduation music. That will be a snap—some of the traditional stuff and a couple of light tunes—a piece of cake. Oh no—I forgot, the Seniors won't be performing with the band; we're in trouble. Twenty-one students are graduating. I'm going to have to call some extra rehearsals just so the band will sound decent. Oh well, that's not so bad, cause as soon as we get that solved, I'm going to have all summer just to enjoy and let my mind be free.

"Whew, that was a close one. I'll just take a couple of moments here to get all the stuff on my desk stacked neatly. What's this? Oh no, it's next year's budget request form. I forgot all about that stupid thing. If I don't fill it out and turn it in, we'll get zip next year. Oh man, look at this, they won't take my budget request until I have a completed inventory attached—that's gonna take three days! No choice, I'll just have to stay a couple of extra days and get it all handled. Some of the students will help. So what's a couple of days when I have three months? No big deal, I can survive it.

"Now let's see, the student's can't come in until Thursday because of the class trip but that will be okay: I'll just spend the first part of that week getting ready for them and doing some of the paper work. Boy, after they have completed all the inventory, I'm off for almost three months. Wow. Wait, I almost forgot music camp at the University starts the second week after the end of school. Seems like I promised them I would serve as a rehearsal assistant to do sectionals. I did. No way I can break that commitment after all they have done for us. It's only a five day camp; we always have some good times and the crew will be there—what's a few more days? Anyway, I've got almost 2-1/2 months of nothing to do coming up. As long as I'm still around by the end of June, I should just wait and check out the annual drum corps show over at the college. There are always lots of creative things to use for next fall. They are always rehearsing a couple of days before, so I'll get some of the band together and we'll go check it out. No big deal—anyway, I've got over two months of open schedule ahead."

"I wonder how many students would hang around two more days so we could march in the July 4th parade? That would sure be a great boost for the band program—and the administration would love it! If we plan to take that big trip next year, we're certainly going to need the community support. Good idea. That will give me a chance to get the new Freshmen involved. We'll meet a couple of days before everyone else to work on the fundamentals. Yeah, it will be worth it. After all, I have the rest of July and August just to lay back and cruise.

This is going to work out fine; just a slight postponement of the vacation. I'll be a better person for seeing this through, and the students will see what true responsibility is all about. Now, I want to get out of town at the end of July: no phones, no mail, just 24 hours a day to do anything I choose. What happens at the end of July? Seems like those dates ring a bell. I know, it's our state bandmaster's convention. This is the year they are having all those great clinicians. I helped set up the program from our region. No choice: if I don't attend and go to our annual breakfast, I'll never hear the end of it. That's not too bad, it will be fun and there is still all of August to jump in the boat and do some serious fishing.

"August . . . August . . . August? Band camp! Oh, my gosh, I almost forgot band camp! Marching band show. I've got to put together the marching band show. Music, flags, and rifles. We haven't had tryouts yet. Wait . . . whoa . . . easy . . . settle down. I'll just make a few phone calls and have some parents help me get that all set. That was a close one; I almost lost it. One week for camp in August and a few days to get some music and write out a drill. I'll hire someone from the college to work with the guard. Solved. That's not so severe; I will still have almost two weeks to spend on the river in complete isolation.

"Oh great: here is next year's football schedule. Now I can see what kind of commitment we are going to have in terms of time. Looks pretty easy. What's this? The first home game is August 22nd. Wait 'til I get my hands on that Athletic Director; school hasn't even started yet. You don't think they expect the band to perform? Of course they do. Well, I just plain won't do it. No, that's not true; I'll do it and so will the band. That leaves me three days between band camp and the pre-school rehearsals. Not much time; it's hardly worth driving out of town. Anyway, that old car isn't good for many more miles. I don't have the money to fly anywhere. Anyway, what is going on during the middle of August that's worth anything? I'll just hang out around here. Wait a minute! Aren't the DCI finals in the middle of August? Yep, just as I thought; I've got it marked down right here. Let's see, it's within a thousand miles of here. You know, I could pile a bunch of the band kids in the car and we could drive straight through both ways and save on a motel. It would be fun! Yeah, let's go for it.

"Hold it—I just gave away my entire vacation. No wonder I never get any free time. Well, this is plain stupid. If that is the way the summer is going to look, I'm going to gather my gear and go fishing right now. I've got two sick days left to use, so it's only fair. If I'm willing to work all summer, the least they can do is give me my sick days.

"Watch out fish, here I come! Now, where is all my fishing equipment? I'll need this tape recorder to play some of the latest promo tapes from the various publishers. And these music educator magazines have been sitting here all year. I'll read some of those, and I should throw in some of this charting paper just in case a creative brainstorm hits me. I'll take my flute too—they say that fish always respond to the sound of a flute. And these index cards of next year's band members—I can memorize the names of the new students while I'm waiting for the fish to bite. I've got a great idea: I'll ask my spouse to join me. Am I still married?"

Moral: "All work and no play makes Jack/Jane a dull director."

Sometimes we have to laugh to keep from crying. We can all relate to the above scenario because we have all fallen into the trap of self-denial when it comes to our time. Somewhere, we must stop and admit the truth: we'll never get all the work done. And the reason is obvious: we are creators, and the very instant one project is completed, we will create another one—and this will go on forever. Free time must also be part of our creation, and to not create it is certain tragedy. The burn-out syndrome will begin to appear and guilt and worry will consume what little relaxation time we do have. Take time, make time; enjoy.

There is no question that the profession demands total commitment. When the end of the school year is at hand, there is a strong need to have a change of scenery. Allow your mind and body a chance to rejuvenate, to put some fresh data in, to avoid the stress and anxiety which can often be a part of the performance schedule. Do yourself the favor of reducing speed for a few days; let your students see there are other priorities in your life. This recharging will do you and the group more good than another month of intense rehearsal. There is no trophy for the director who spends 24 hours, 7 days a week in the band, choir, or whatever room. There are countless rewards for the director who has a grasp of the need for variety in life. Cash in. Don't wait another three years when you can afford to take the time—take it now. We are creatures of habit—develop a positive habit of personal enjoyment time.

The amount of research I have done on what makes people successful could fill a library wall, and there is one commonality that serves as a basic theme for all of them: they take time for themselves. Whether it is an avid hobby or annual retreat, they all create personal time. Perhaps it's not a matter of getting away from it all as much as it is a situation of getting next to it all. In other words, when we are out of sorts with ourselves, our entire environment reflects this uncertainty. We all need time to get in touch with ourselves.

As you head into this special time of year, build in some time for you. Do some new things for the first time ever; create some time where you don't have to accomplish anything; complete one of those childhood wishes you never had the chance to do; visit with some new people; get lost in some goofy project; really look at a summer sunset; play in the rain—and on, and on.

Sounds good, doesn't it? So let's go, let's have some fun. Are you ready? I'll be with you as soon as I find my keys. Now let me see, where did I put those *!-%!* keys? I just had them right here. Oh no, it had the School Master Key on the ring! I'm not even supposed to have one of those. One of those kids has ripped off my keys. I'm gonna get fired for sure unless I find those keys. Wait. Remember. I put them in the inside pocket of my sports coat. Thank heaven, that was a close one. Now where did I put my sports coat? I just had it last week. Oh no, it also had my end of the year check in the pocket and my billfold was in there too! Stop. I remember. I took it to the cleaners. I'll just run down there and pick it up and everything will be a-O.K.! Now, which cleaners was it? Yes, I remember; everything's going to be just fine. Here we are,

I'll just run in and pick it up and then I'm free. There's a sign on the door: what does it say? "Closed for the Summer—Gone Fishin'!"

Don't let this happen to you. Never lose your keys to success: take control.

*"Opportunities always look
better going than coming."*

# Benefits Beyond
# Revenue via Fund
# Raising Thank-You's

It all began last spring when a former student called to tell me he had just received an official invitation to have his high school band perform in the prestigious Rose Bowl Parade. What an honor! After the enthusiastic exchanges of congratulations, he started telling me of his plan for raising the necessary funds for the trip and of the busy schedule ahead right up to the step-off of the parade on January 1st. As always, he was well-organized in his thoughts and plans for the upcoming months. This could well be one of the main reasons the band received this coveted invitation in the first place.

Through the remainder of the school year and starting in the fall, the band's monthly newsletter faithfully reported the upcoming performance in addition to all of the interesting band news. One day the mail delivered a wonderfully written letter from the director explaining a raffle which would include two round trip tickets to the parade with all the extras as part of the package. The band was to receive all the proceeds as part of their continuing effort to achieve the financial goal needed to make the trip. This seemed like an appropriate way to offer personal accolades to the group, the director, and all those affiliated with the program. It wasn't the chance to win a free trip which caught my eye, but rather the way it was presented. It offered an opportunity to participate and support these young musicians who had chosen to commit to a high level of performance both on and off the parade route. A small check for the raffle tickets was sent with well wishes for success in their important endeavor.

Up to this point, there is nothing unusual about the scenario. It is a standard operating procedure annually for many bands. Though the Rose Bowl Parade is a once-in-a-lifetime opportunity, that is not the case with the hard work and fund raising which goes with any trip: new uniform purchase, extended instrument budget, etc. You name it and there is probably some type of outside subsidy needed, and this means wise planning and intelligent strategy.

However the story now takes a different twist. The return mail produced a very gracious thank-you letter, the stubs from the raffle tickets, and a hand-written note of appreciation on the bottom of the letter. In fact, there was even a message wishing me good luck in the drawing and an update on the band's progress. Winning the trip meant little to me, but the unusual and welcomed communication was a refreshing shift from the normal procedure of many years of contributions.

Several weeks later came yet another personal letter, and the announcement of the trip winner. Again, there was a personal message and a thank-you for my participation. Much education was happening in this process. This was far more than just a fund-raising project. Of course the VCR was running the day of the parade and it was personally satisfying to see the exemplary performance of the band as they made their way across the television screen down Pasadena Boulevard with their heads held high. A job well done, but the story goes on.

The next day, two post cards were awaiting me in the mailbox. One was from a drill team member and the second from one of the instrumentalists in the band. The hand-written cards, appropriately spotlighting the Rose Bowl stadium, had a California postmark. Each card had a thank-you note and a few choice words about the positive experience the band was enjoying.

In truth, more revenue might have been spent on postage for the thank-you notes and letters than the initial donation, but the implication of what this says about the program is beyond mea-sure. It all represents an outgrowth of the basic value of appreciation. How many times have we extended ourselves on behalf of someone or some organization and then not heard from the source until the next time of need? Certainly nobody expects anything in return for helping out. If so, then it is a form of manipulation, but isn't it exciting when someone does take the time to share that simple but powerful message: *Thank you. You made a difference.*

There is something else about all of this. When it is time for the band to take on their next venture, or buy some needed equipment, my intentions to help are going to be very favorable. They have helped pave the way for the future bands in their school. Certainly others who were part of this bandwagon must feel the same. Not only did we help, but we were acknowledged and appreciated for our help.

The members of the group also learned an important lesson of life: "We're only worth what we give away." They took the time to make every contributor feel important, cared for, needed, and a fundamental reason the project was a success. What a gift. Do you suppose this would work in each and every part of life? If we acknowledged people for their efforts, would they continue to participate and offer genuine support? Of course they would...we all would.

Just when you think you know it all, someone comes along and adds an obvious benefit to a traditional game which gives it new life and meaning. I can tell you one old dog who learned some new tricks. Maybe your band already has such a follow-up program for your patrons, volunteers, and all your contributors. If so, keep it going and growing. If not, maybe it is time to incorporate this in your future plans. We're all concerned about the welfare of our band programs and here is a way to garner support from all those who love a parade. That includes everyone in your community, doesn't it? *Strike Up The Band*—and have some band logo thank-you notes printed at the same time.

# Part Five

# Thoughts About Competition

# Thoughts about Competition

Competition is a common topic of conventions, late night band director's conversations, and countless articles of "pro and con" written in every publication from the beginning of time. It is particularly keen in our education world because it always requires an opinion. Wherever there is one set of thoughts, there are certain to be a set of "counter-thoughts."

Perhaps we all have to decide for ourselves whether we favor competition or don't favor it, and regardless of our thoughts, I'm not sure any of it will change the course of the world. It appears it is not a "yes or no" situation, but one of how we deal with it. It can certainly be defended on either side of the fence with a high degree of "absoluteness," yet there is evidence to offset even the most avid proponent.

We have all witnessed the program of complete avoidance of competition, and seen remarkable results. However, we have all experienced fine programs where the entire format is built on competition...and have seen remarkable results. It is living proof of the old adage, "It is not what you do, but how you do it."

It is ironic that the more we understand about this, the more confusing our opinions can become. The following section will give you the opportunity to become more confused. After many years of participation in both camps, I find that it is certain that I am uncertain. Enjoy!

*"The rung of a ladder was never meant to rest upon, but only to hold a man's weight long enough to enable him to put the other somewhat higher."*
—*Thomas Huxley*

# Let's Band Together!

Is music a competitive sport? Who stands to gain when pitting one musical organization against another? Are music education programs falling into the trap of being geared to competition seasons much like athletics? Where does one draw the line when it comes to the "we-gotta-win" attitude? As a band director, music teacher, conveyor of art, is the final evaluation based on some subjective rating from a local contest? What is the future of music in the schools?

The answer to all these questions? There is no answer. You must answer each of these for yourself—and your answer will support your own philosophies and beliefs. If we polled 100 band directors, you can rest assured that we would end up with 106 different sets of answers. You can count on at least a half dozen of them to change their minds in the middle of the response.

Everyone has concerns when it comes to the future of our music education programs. We all have that in common; anything that appears to threaten its growth and development should be monitored with a watchful eye. Knowing that the welfare of our art is of prime interest, lets look a the contest scene and what implications it has on our organizations, our students, our teachers, and the direction we are headed.

208

Today's seasonal contest schedules look something like this: September, October, November: Marching Band Contest; December, January, February: Color Guard Contest, Solo/Ensemble contest, Drill Team Contest; March, April: Playing Contest, Jazz Band Contest——May, June: Spring Marching/Concert/Jazz Contest; July, August: Summer Camps. Not to mention the regular set of music responsibilities from basketball games, community request performances, to the back-up music for the annual frog jump. It seems endless—it is endless.

Have we created a no-win situation by putting such a heavy burden on ourselves and our profession? Are band directors throwing in the towel because the demands of the schedule combined with the pressure to win are simply impossible to meet? How do you feel? Are we losing perspective of what music is supposed to contribute to a young person's life? It all seems to boil down to the focus of your teaching. If you feel that competition is harmful to your purpose, then don't compete. Put your energies to another area of your program. Perhaps you are interested in hosting several guest conductors during your concert season; the learning potential of an exchange concert with a neighboring school; a field trip to expose your student to a major symphony orchestra; or an in-house workshop with a professional performer. Waste no time pointing out the pitfalls of any other system. Use your enthusiasm to create situations where positive, forward progress can be attained by your students. Others may see the competitive arena in a far different light:

- The chance for my students to be evaluated by someone other than me.
- Seeing and hearing others, and being able to exchange knowledge.
- Getting to know ourselves better in a situation outside of school.
- Developing our talents as musicians and ambassadors for our community.
- Creating a family goal for our group, our school, our parents.

This attitude will produce the same predictable positives. Two groups entering any competition, of any kind, can come away with totally different reactions, all based on their preconceived notions of what the results will bring. Music teachers are prime examples of the self-fulfilling prophecy. Your desires and/or fears are reflected by everyone who touches your program.

Competition is a very potent experience. It can make or break a person. There is grave concern that too much competition can distort the purpose of music education; that it redirects the emphasis of teaching time and teacher's goals. For some, this concern is well-founded. Square pegs will never fit into round holes To those who have discovered the benefits of competition, step back and as objectively as possible judge your product with the critical eyes of any fine teacher.

Fine tuning at this level is a must. We all seem to take sides, jump to conclusions, assume steadfast positions, leap to our soapboxes; yet the knowledge we have is usually derived from only one-sided opinions of the question at hand. When you communicate with someone who is adamant about his or her thoughts, ask if the opposing view has been personally experienced or simply dismissed through hearsay. There's a marvelous Indian proverb that says: "Never judge a man before you walk a mile in his moccasins." How blunt, how true; how guilty we are. Music education needs our mutual efforts. Let's pool our talents, our thoughts in supporting our young musicians in the best way we can. The way you answered the questions at the beginning of this chapter will be exactly right for you, just as alternative answers will be right for your colleagues; but the answers may not be the same. Thank goodness! The variety you will bring to music education is its life blood: Strike Up The Band!

*"The credit belongs to the man who is actually in the arena, whose face is marred by dust and sweat and blood; who strives valiantly; who errs and comes short again and again, who knows the great enthusiasms, the great devotions, and spends himself in a worthy cause; who at the best, knows the triumph of high achievement; and who, at the worst, if he fails, at least fails while daring greatly, so that his place shall never be with those timid souls who know neither victory nor defeat."*
— *Theodore Roosevelt*

# The Value Of Risking

Performance after performance, band after band, you are going to witness one of the nation's most outstanding events as Bands of America presents the 19XX Grand National Championship. Any spectator, regardless how knowledgeable, must sit in awe of what is being accomplished by young people who have chosen to dedicate their time and energy to the team goal of a quality production. Bravo!

This offers us, the audience, an opportunity to support this quest for excellence by cheering on each and every student who has chosen to go the distance in this spotlight of honor. Yes, it is a competition—and you can be assured each performer, staff member, parent, administrator, and director is playing to win. Certainly they would not have reached this level if they had any intention of being less than first place, whether in reality or fantasy. Even those who know there is literally no possibility of standing in the winner's circle, or even making the top twelve, secretly believe there may be an outside chance they could pull off the ultimate upset. That feeling, that hope, is the essence of competition.

We, the entertained, must honor this choice by expanding our winners circle to include each and every young person. We do this by cheering every band knowing, in our hearts, they all deserve first place just for being out there. Rest assured, you are seeing 110% effort on the part of everyone involved.

Let us make sure we reflect that same energy level. It's not about "this" band vs. "that" band, or if "Band A" outperformed "Band B." That kind of thinking turns the whole event into a sport—an either/or event. Rather, it is about teaching young guys and gals the value of risking: of reaching beyond their known potential, stretching to grasp that next rung of the ladder. Some will achieve; others will fall short. As supporters, we can play a vital role in this experience by seeing to it their "short fall" has a soft landing; and that the "fall" serves as a personal growth experience and an incentive to jump back up and get right back in the game, knowing there has been a tremendous measure of self-improvement gained through the process.

Every person involved in this musical spectacular is a winner. That fact was established when each group chose to participate. Yes, you too. If you were not the best of the best, this program would not be in your hands right now. The responsibility of setting the standard of championship behavior is on your shoulders. The audience serves as the role models for everyone. Let's pledge ourselves to this end: a class act. Sportsmanship and common support must be top priority in attaining this most worthwhile goal. Without it, what could be a significant educational experience might well become a negative charge for those involved. You count. You determine the success for all.

We are blessed to live in a country where band is part of the daily curriculum. Add to this the countless hours of volunteer help donated by staff, parents, communities, and students to bring this all to fruition. And there is no way to measure the amount of caring sharing and personal love given through each and every hour of preparation. It takes a winning attitude to get this point. Let's all band together to exemplify this attitude so that every young person will feel the value of risking.

"To go forward in the face of overwhelming odds is to risk failure. But risks must be taken because the greatest hazard in life is to risk nothing. The person who risks nothing, does nothing, has nothing, is nothing, He may avoid suffering and sorrow, but he cannot learn, feel changes, trust, grow, or love. Chained by his certitudes, he is a slave. He has given up his freedom. Only a person who takes risks is truly free . . ." (reference?)

It is so much more than a marching band contest, a competition, a comparing of performances. It is a chance to know what it takes to achieve success in life. We all serve as teachers in this endeavor. Let the class begin—strike up the band!

# Creating Winners

Another school year is initiated and every band-choir-orchestra director has carefully marked the calendar with the various performance dates for the upcoming academic year. Every attempt to avoid conflicts with track meets, SAT testing, student government conventions, and spring proms has been made. "Let the games begin!"

As we begin, let us take a moment to highlight some of the basic principles we can share with the students through our musical talents. Although we are interested in correct notes, accurate counting, phrasing, dynamics, etc., we also must focus on our responsibility to share fundamental guidelines to living which can adapt to each and every part of life. Herein, lies the secret of the master teacher who makes a positive difference in the life of each student.

Let's focus this article on the concept of winning. Competition is such an integral part of our society and we have seen it grow in our musical activities with the increase of local and national festivals across the country.

Although many people have very strong pro or con opinions about the value of competition, it is deeply rooted within our educational system, from report cards to making the varsity athletic team. We have auditions for chair placement, who sings the solo, organizational officers, awards at the annual banquet, and so forth. In this living lab, we have a perfect opportunity to develop a healthy and productive attitude of winning, and also define (through role modeling) the behavior of a winner. This is most easily accomplished by comparing the actions of a winner and a loser. Of course, what we must keep in mind is: winning and losing are merely labels to identify the way we handle various situations. Let's be clear that winning and first place are not necessarily synonymous. Likewise, losing and last place do not mean the same thing. With the emphasis in our society on number 1, it is easy for students—as well as many adults—to conclude: "Unless we are first place, we are losers."

This logic leads to the accompanying behavior of a loser. And we all know the loser's attitude is one of much frustration and low productivity. This ultimately leads to giving up—quitting. At this point, we have little chance of educating if the child is no longer in the class. With this in mind, here are some trademarks of winners and losers, and ideas we can share with our students to insure they will always win in every endeavor.

## 1. DEALING WITH MISTAKES
Mistakes are a part of life. Each day is a series of trial and error, and the successful people are the ones who can make the best of each and every situation. Losers are interested in justifying an error. They will explain and explain why something doesn't work. They can communicate in detailed terms what went wrong and how it went wrong, and why they weren't at fault. Winners will take the mistake as a sign to correct and will immediately go about making the necessary adjustments. They are solution-oriented, and realize the value of moving quickly to avoid the hold-up of the entire operation. Identifying a flat tire and the cause of the mishap rarely gets the car back on the road—change the tire.

## 2. SETTING A GOAL FOR EVERY ACTIVITY
An individual with a winning attitude will achieve excellence regardless of the price they have to pay or regardless how trivial the task. They are incredibly persistent, self-motivated, and do not accept the standards of others, but set their own standards. They always produce—always! Losers seem to fall short of every goal they set. When this happens, they tend to bolster their own sagging self-image by blaming other people and circumstances for shortcomings. They always know why everything doesn't work, but

rarely have much to contribute to solving the problems at hand. Music is such a great avenue for short and long term goal setting. There are so many opportunities to produce and recognize excellence, from beginning scales to concertos.

### 3. UNDERSTANDING GIVE AND TAKE

A true winner knows real victory comes from giving to other people. They see that the value in learning, acquiring, developing, and growing is to share it with others. They think in terms of we-us rather than I-me. Their behavior is always caring, open, and non-selfish. Losers are always skeptical and suspicious. They feel if anyone finds out what they know, it could be used against them, therefore they spend much of their energy closing-off, hiding, and creating barriers so others will be confused. So much of music education can demonstrate the benefits of giving: performance, rehearsals, extra effort, teaching others, sharing parts—simply making the behavior of a winner a habit.

### 4. VALUE OF COMPETITION

A winner realizes the benefits of competition are not in the final comparisons, but in the self-growth gained in the preparation and the competition experience. They see competition as a game, and not as an all-or-nothing determination of any kind of self-worth. They play the game at 110% energy level and find great personal satisfaction in playing as opposed to making the value of the game the results—the score. Losers will pretend they really don't want to win; therefore, if they lose they have a perfect excuse: "I didn't really care in the first place; if I really cared, I could have won." Music presents so many instances we can use to support personal growth. Each day offers a chance to better our discipline, from sitting straight in the chair to recognizing every key change. Every rehearsal and performance can represent a victory if we recognize it—and use more winning habits.

### 5. THE GIFT OF CHOICE

Each moment of each day, we have to make choices. Choosing to be in music is such an important choice. These are the students who go the extra mile. Winners understand they have to be responsible for choosing how to invest their time, spend their energy, and determine their attitude. They operate knowing there is no need to be in a musical organization, and that it is a privilege to have the choice to join. They honor and respect their choice. Losers tend to feel they are trapped in the group, and that the group should be dedicated to making them happy. Of course, they continue to display a weak attitude so the group is forced to give them attention.

Music can represent a perfect situation for acknowledgment of positive contribution. It can be an arena for finding the good in each and every participant. We can make it very fashionable to be a winner. Of course these attributes can apply to each and every part of life. As music teachers, we have a prime opportunity to develop these qualities via every teaching experience. We can make a difference when this becomes the philosophical foundation to our life-contribution, sometimes called a job, but so much more than that.

It would be wonderful if all students went on to play and sing throughout their lives, but we all know how the instruments and choir robes find their way to the attic. However, each student will go on to become a working member of society. Knowing this , it seems crucial we continue to bring out the best in all of them and give them the guidelines to success which will apply to anything they choose in life. Let's dedicate our energies to creating winners. Here's to a great year of many victories.

*"Our chief want in life is somebody
who will make us do what we can."*
—*Ralph Waldo Emerson*

# Winning: A Matter of Context and Choice

Too often, people confuse winning with first place. You must understand that a person (or group) might get first place and not win, and certainly could win and not end up in first place. This all sounds philosophically confusing but read on, it could make a great difference in the way you approach everything that you do.

How many times have you watched a group perform a stunning routine and come in second or third in the final rankings? How many times have you witnessed a powerhouse, consistently first-place champion accept the second place trophy because there was one group just an ever-so-slight degree more "on" during their performance, giving them the edge in the final score? How many times have you felt robbed because of some minor error in performance that you really had no control over? We have all seen and been a part of all these instances—plus a host of others. People have disguised award names, class, divisions, contest titles, etc., trying to avoid making anyone the loser.

Perhaps we're tackling the problem from the wrong angle. Suppose I told you that winning simply meant putting out 100% effort during your performance, and that the satisfaction that you would receive—the real reward—was going to be that split-second instant at the completion of your performance: you know, the one where you feel like your heart is going to jump out of your throat and your spine gets all tingly. If that's what winning was supposed to be, and nothing more, then you would really not care where you ended up in the competition. You see, you would have already won prior to any announcement of placement.

Now what is really important to you: are you interested in the personal satisfaction of winning, or are you interested in getting first place? Reread that last question—answer truthfully. If you spend your entire life striving for first place and being disappointed when it does not come your way, you can count on a constant uphill battle well sown with many heartbreaks ahead. On the other hand, if you are concerned with what you will obtain from winning, then you begin tackling the whole problem with a different set of objectives—and you can be assured you will have the chance to win at everything that you do, along with many others like you.

It's great to be a winner, and it's great to win every time you go for it. The choice is really up to each of us. It's regrettable to see any group put out their very finest effort only to meet with head-on disappointment due to some mystical value that we have attached to a first place trophy determined by a totally subjective panel of subject-to human-error judges. Too often, evaluations on the part of both students and directors in terms of the group's worth are based on these rankings. Feelings that range from total failure to hostility can be seen at the announcement of the final scores. It means all the joy and fulfillment that comes from the dedication and excitement of working together for a common cause are over-shadowed by some flashy trophy or title. There is little credit to any contest that produces only one winner and several losers, when in fact it has the ability to produce all winners. Directors who support the idea of winning must carefully lay the groundwork so that all the members of the group share the same philosophy of what winning is and what it can mean to the future. The rankings then become an extra-added-attraction, and only coincidental to the wealth of the rewards that come from the experience of doing your best. A trophy of victory can be seen in the eyes of a winner; and only there. It can only be described by those of us who have many of them stored in our bank of memories; and they can be shared with everyone for a lifetime. A trophy from a store sits on a shelf only to gather dust: its life is short; its value is meaningful only to the owner. A friend of mine once told me, "Never let any of your groups be deceived by the popular cheer `We're Number 1,' because if you really are, you won't have to tell anyone—they'll all know it." Winning and first place are only the same if you let them be the same; the choice is yours.

*"If we work upon marble, it will perish;*
*if we work upon brass, time will efface it...*
*but if we work upon immortal minds,*
*we engrave on those tablets something*
*which will brighten all eternity."*
*—Daniel Webster*

# How To Separate Winning From 1st Place

To all who believe winning is an important part of any band program, I want you to look at some truths that may not have been at the forefront of your thinking. We all have heard the seemingly endless argument that goes on about the value—and lack of value—of competition, whether it be in a solo-ensemble festival or a national championship title. There have been countless variations of scoresheets and rating scales to accommodate every philosophy from "let everyone be in first place," to "there can be only one number 1."

The fact of the matter is: we are all competitive in some ways— even the guy who competitively defends his position that he's not into competition. (What a "Catch-22" paradox!) Perhaps attitudes vary on the benefits that can be derived from competition; it seems, however, that the people who have a negative view of the activity are those who have never participated with a Sure-Win Attitude (the key phrase here).

Those who are winning are supportive of any situation where

an evaluation of their product is available—in essence, a competition. Therefore, it stands to reason that all those who stand the chance to win will find a way to participate and expose their students to the self-development that comes from going for it.

Let's spotlight the high school marching band and use that group as our example, but be aware that it applies to every group in your program. Do you compete with your marching band? Why? If your answer was yes, the second part of the question was probably easy and fun to answer. If you answered "no," you may find yourself trying to justify your answer in terms of the evils of the competitive arena.

Are you speaking from experience or from theories that support your beliefs? If you could be assured a victory in a national level competition; if you knew that your band would sense the thrills that come from being a winner; if you were certain you could make all of these benefits available to your students through participation; would you compete? Is it the desire of winning, or the fear of losing that holds you back? Winning is possible at any time, if you can separate winning from first place. First places mean no more or no less than the value that you give them. Knowing this, and knowing that sooner or later you will come into a situation where you can't be first place, I wonder why people attach such sacred value to it. Eventually we all lose at something.

Winning, on the other hand, is an attitude that can be directly applied to everything we do in life. Its value can be drawn upon all the time. How does one learn winning (sure-winning) through competition? It develops through the understanding that real satisfaction comes from the participation in the process of the game, rather than concentrating on first place. Sure-winners know that not getting first place is inevitable, so they win by not putting a lot of philosophical value on it. Winning then becomes knowing your situation and being confident about it.

Nothing can undo that kind of self-assurance. The process and the goals, therefore, become one so that it is impossible to lose. Think this one through. If your goal is to win by going through the process of participation and you admit that no one can determine the shifting factors of the unknown that make a first place position certain, you have created a situation where you can win—or your band can win--every time For those of you who have never been in first place and find yourself discouraged and somewhat threatened by the word competition, let's take a hard, cold look at what it takes to be number 1.

It's very feasible that you may not be interested in a first place victory, but may want to focus on another part of winning. What is first place? Being Number 1 means that you are no longer "one of the gang," enjoying the camaraderie and friendship of working together to knock off the champ. You are somewhat isolated and, sooner or later, your friends become your opponents, challenging your top dog position.

Those who have been there will be quick to tell you that first place is lonely. You or your band become the standard which everyone uses as the one to go for; they are all out to unseat you. For many, first place is a burden that casts a spell of undue anxiety until the relief of being replaced comes around. People who are always at odds about not getting first place will not win once they do achieve it. They cannot see that a win at all costs attitude will create more pressure for them when they do get to first place; they still will not have won because they will be so busy defending their hallowed first place against all oncomers that they'll turn their winning opportunity into defeat by failing to look at the self-improvement and growth they gained through the process of participation. See what happened: they lost by being in first place. Those kinds of winners never win at anything. They build in their own self-defeat, their own lack of confidence will not allow them to experience victory. People who doubt the value of competition doubt themselves. They have failed to see that every situation provides an opportunity for positive self-growth. Every apparent failure is a chance to correct and improve. Evaluation of your band creates support for the growth of your students, your program, and most of all, you. It is the motivation force that can turn any program into a success. You have the chance to see just how much fun band directing can be: the opportunity to win at your chosen work in life. We all have the ability to redirect the way we compete and to learn from our past failures. Self-evaluation and the extent to which we use it as a result of competition will determine the opportunities for our future.

*"Those who dream by night in the dusty recesses of their minds wake in the day to find that all was vanity; but the dreamers of the day are dangerous men, for they may act their dreams with open eyes and make it possible."*

—*T.E. Lawrence*

# Six Steps to Better Competition Scores

I support the competition aspect of the marching band world; it can contribute significantly to a young person's life and, without a doubt, can create immeasurable visibility to any band program. The positive effects of this level of participation serve as an example of the power of youth and the tremendous potential that this kind of teamwork projects. Having spent many years directing band, and now serving as a judge for numerous contests, I feel it is my responsibility to share some thoughts with you concerning the band's overall performances as it relates to your job as band director.

Marching bands today are improving at an unbelievable rate. From the musical expansion of the percussion section to the breath-taking visual contribution of the auxiliary groups, the marching band has come into its own. Stadiums are packed full of band fans ready to enthusiastically cheer on the hometown favorite at the contest of the year. As a band director, you will find that being a part of this kind of event produces rewards not only for the band, but for you as well. The personal satisfaction that comes from going for it is as thrilling as being the football coach at the state finals.

It is here that my concern arises, and it is here that I think we all should move with utmost care and caution, always focusing on the welfare of the student. Look at your marching band carefully and evaluate your teaching. Following is a list of six common problems that keep sending up red flares to that little music education person that lives in my conscience. Do yourself and your band a favor and evaluate your program to be sure you are avoiding these common errors.

### Problem 1. Basic tone production.

*How identified:* The band sounds top heavy and very thin. This usually means second and third parts are not being played in balance with the first part. Lack of proper breath support and proper tone focus hampers projection.

*Solution:* No easy solution! It is just many hours of teaching on a one-to-one or small class situation. The rule to remember is: "There is no such thing as too much breath support." Good fundamental teaching is required.

### Problem 2. Weak percussion writing and resultant poor musical contribution.

*How identified:* The obvious tell-tale sign is that the band has no punch. Both the top and the bottom are lost from the dynamic scale. One struggles to hear phrasing and cadence points. The group can't swing without this vital percussion support.

*Solution:* Attention must be given to the section. Don't turn them loose on their own and then complain when they don't play well. This is your greatest dynamic and stylistic catalyst and it needs your constant guidance. Work with the percussion section not in spite of them. A real luxury is having a percussion instructor or competent section leader to work hand-in-hand with you.

### Problem 3. A guard (Auxiliary) that is tacked on (added as an afterthought) to the back of the drill.

*How identified:* Visually it is a dead giveaway because the form is usually complete without the auxiliary. They always are on the perimeter of the design and if they do move into the group it appears forced and awkward.

*Solution:* Think of the guard as part of the band" Strive to Achieve visual harmony in both the drill and the routine. When writing the show, consult with the person who is in charge of this group. The integration of the auxiliary within the drill significantly strengthens your entire show impact.

### Problem 4. Musicians who have no understanding of style.

*How identified:* The group avoids extremes in style (e.g., march, jazz, disco, Latin, etc.); they all tend to sound alike. The stylistic nuances that are such a vital part of selling each production are simply not there. The players do not understand the interpretation of the idiomatic rhythm problems and phrases as they relate to the given style.

*Solution:* Expose the students to listening opportunities that will serve as a model for their ears, not just yours. If you are playing Mangione, be certain that they understand his concept by listening to his records; the same is true with all other styles. The best of each style is not too extreme

### Problem 5. The lack of woodwind utilization.

*How identified:* This is an easy one: it means the woodwinds are always staged in the back on the extreme sides, and that their musical contribution is minimal. The all-brass sound is dominant and the beautiful woodwind timbre avoided rather than utilized.
*Solution:* The solution is obvious: *use them.* Choose music with woodwind features. Don't be afraid to stage them in front to capture their gorgeous tonal contribution. Don't consider them extra baggage. Quite the contrary: use them as a fine painter would use pastels for subtle shadings.

As competitions grow, and as more of you become active, it is important that we all take just a moment now and then to objectively review the basics. Any band that is solid on the above five points is an excellent group and would definitely be a top contender in any competition. When all is said and done, it comes down to having a fundamental working knowledge of teaching music fundamentals and a keen eye at adapting it to a visual interpretation. This is another way of saying, "There's no short cut!" I extend my sincere congratulations to all of you who are creating these superb bands that we see everywhere from coast to coast—and a very special vote of support and confidence to all of you who are building your band programs.

Oh yes, there's one other thing: I know that there is no place on the judge's sheet to evaluate the attitude of the students, but I think I speak for many of us when I say that any student who takes the field in competition is a winner. You are making a significant contribution.

*"Most of us think less of ourselves than we really are; what we think is less than what we know; what we know is less than what we love.; and what we love is less than what there is; and, to that precise extent, are much less than what we are!"*

# A Posture of Success

We have all witnessed outstanding groups that simply take our breath away, and also have observed some performances which seem to be void of any breath of life. The keys to success for any performance would fill a library: proper tone production, positioning of the instruments for appropriate staging, supportive color contrasts in terms of guard equipment/uniforms/flags, etc., balanced instrumentation, tension-release factors of the visual and musical program, matched footwear, matched marching styles, stylistic interpretation, interpretation of horn focus, focusing the energy for highlights, highlighting the appropriate sections, productive sectionals in rehearsal, proper rehearsal techniques—and on, and on, and on.

How easy it is for all of us to get lost in this seemingly endless maze of confusion. Where do we start? What one thing can we do which is certain to make a our groups better? Something which can be transferred to every facet of our total program? One of my most respected friends is commonly called upon to work with various bands (and corps) because he seems to perform magic with any organization. Having observed him in action, it is quickly apparent he never really changes anything, but simply upgrades what the students already have learned by creating a common denominator for everything they do. Although he calls it pride, that may be for the benefit of the group dynamics; it really is a *performance-posture filter*. From loading the bus to selling the final climax of the show, everything is part of the performance posture. This simple premise, as we all know, is often overlooked in our urgency to get more content into the show.

CONTEXT vs. CONTENT, or HOW WE DO WHAT WE DO IS ALWAYS MORE IMPRESSIVE THAN WHAT WE DO.

A case of back to the basics, as often proclaimed by the wise veterans who have seen it all, and are well aware of the importance of fundamentals. There is no substitute for the Cardinal Laws of the Ages which were shouted from the front of the classroom in Marching Band 101, as well as in our first day of elementary band: "Sit up straight, put your feet flat on the floor, and don't let your instrument droop. Always be sure you have good posture." To this day, I can hear Mr. Gombert's predictable words of caution at the beginning of each rehearsal: "Are you in your proper performance posture?"

If it is so simple, so apparent, so obvious, it should be a given for everyone. There is no question about it: it should. It controls our opinion and judgements. Examine your own thoughts and feelings the next time you are in an audience observing a performance. Are you not affected by the way the performers enter, their presence even when they are not the focal point, their mannerisms, their energy? Of course you are. The very word, *perform*, means per-the-form, to become a part of the form, or, in this case, to be in total support of the theme's intended communication to the audience. Anything which is out of the form or detracts from the form violates or destroys the shape of the intended posture. One cannot hide or come on and off stage at his or her convenience.

Having the performers (with-the-form-ers) understand this concept or reality opens up new frontiers of possibility for the entire organization. We have all watched the two percussionists carry on an extended conversation during the clarinet solo. It's not a case of premeditated mutiny: they simply aren't aware they are still in-the-form, therefore they have relaxed their performance posture. On the marching band field, it is not uncommon to be enjoying a fantastic visual move appropriately embellishing the musical phrase, only to have our attention drawn to one flutist with instrument dangling as she watches the ground unaware of her crucial importance to the overall picture. What a grand teaching opportunity to let her know she counts: she has worth; She matters. And if done in the proper context, everyone in the group will stand a bit taller, not to mention the boost in this young lady's self-esteem.

This exciting issue of time is a priceless compilation of information and expertise from the most creative and insightful designers our activity has ever known. There is not a source book for much of this data, for it is created as the ink hits the page. However, let us not deceive ourselves into thinking once we have the masterfully designed drill, our final goal has been achieved; this common trap is analogous to the naive young director who concludes that by having his or her group play "Lincolnshire Posy," the band will then be in the same company with the Eastman Wind Ensemble. A ludicrous form of logic; everyone agrees. It is equally as inappropriate from a design vantage point; having a sixty-piece high school band attempt to duplicate the drill demands of the Santa Clara Vanguard is a negative growth experience for everyone. They simply cannot handle this kind of demand. It will break their backs, for they do not have the strength or posture to bear this burden. Please, one step at a time with proper posture.

Our friend Webster describes posture as a way of carrying or positioning oneself. A mode or a status. An attitude or a tendency. To assume a pose for an effect. This could well be a description of what is intended via visual design. The purpose is to position our players in such a way that we recreate the attitude of the musical expression through the imaged field-performance to achieve a calculated effect. The more successful we are, the better the effect. In a realistic sense, visual design and posture are one-in-the-same, which means that without proper posture we are certain to lose the integrity of the design. The proof of this logic can be easily confirmed when enjoying the finest examples of our art. The dignity of their posture is consuming. Their first impression predicts the certain-to-be stellar performance to come.

In conclusion, let me go back to a bit of advice a friend gave to one of his colleagues in the middle of a discussion about the lack of sufficient rehearsal time and the proverbial frustration over too much to do and too little time to do it. "But we don't have enough time in the practice to spend any of it working on the fundamentals! We just can't afford it!" And my talented friend replied with firm gentleness, "Your plight is no different than most. The truth is: you can't afford not to. Without proper posture in your band, you are doomed to mediocrity regardless of the music, drills, or whatever else you bring to them." After a few moments of tense silence, the band director smiled and shook hands with his wise mentor. Education is a life-long process. Enjoy the knowledge this publication has to offer, add it to your library of understanding, then let's all go to work keeping in mind, as Mr. Gombert would say, we are in our proper performance posture. Strike up the band.

*"If at first you don't succeed, you are normal."*

# The Real Value:
# It's Up to You

A special message must go out to band directors and students who choose to participate in any competitive activity. In addition to understanding all the rules and regulations of the program, one must also understand that there is a fundamental rule—not written anywhere—which overrides all other rules and really is the determining factor in the success or failure of your performance: the adjudicator's decisions are subjective.

From the French horn soloist judge at the local music festival to the referee at a professional basketball game, any decision is based on that judge's opinion given the circumstances at the moment. If it were a black and white choice, we would create a very efficient machine to do it. Knowing this, it should seem obvious that any outcome of any competition would bear the same characteristics:

1) opinionated
2) slanted in favor of the judge's background
3) influenced by past experience
4) subject to human error and a host of other data that is all based on this one fact: everyone is inadequate at something.

How seriously do you take the results of a competition? Now don't confuse the results with the experience of the event: that's only one very small part of the whole. If you put any measurable significance on the outcome of your score, you have just voided the chance to put the emphasis on the outcome of the experience. The success of your efforts is in the :

1) creating
2) planning
3) practicing
4) solving the problems along the way
5) growth and development of the people involved
6) personal rewards in sharing everything while achieving your common goals, and
7) the final performance—*not the score.*

Who knows whether your efforts were a success better than you? Certainly not a person who sees the final product for the first time. No one knows how far you've progressed except you and your group.

## THE VALUE OF OPINION (SCORES)

After several years on both sides of the fence—as a band director, as a judge, and as a fierce competitor—there is one haunting fact that I see cropping up at every competitive event: we all tend to lose perspective of what this is really supposed to mean to us as educators. The final score is often interpreted as carved-in-stone law that will determine the future of one's life. If you let someone else's opinion carry that much influence, you and your program will be guided by the slightest whim of anyone who comments on your efforts.

We learn by listening to others, but if the input is non-applicable, inaccurate in terms of your circumstances, non-supportive of your goals, misdirected, or whatever, simply dismiss it. Challenging an opinion is a losing battle; even if you do sway someone to your side of an issue, it just reinforces how invalid the opinion was to begin with.

## COMPETITION IS A GAME

Competition in anything is a game created by all of us to draw attention to our product. It is a mythological spotlight which carries as much real value as each of us choose to give it. It can be thrilling, nerve-wracking, rewarding, painful, chaotic, even enlightening. It can be whatever we choose it to be. Simply keep in mind that it is a game, and it is only meaningful to the people who are participating. It's often hard to believe, but no one else really cares! Who is the nation's top pinochle player? You see? Ask any pinochle advocate. Then be prepared to hear opinion after opinion—and when it's all said and done, it still won't change anything.

Supposedly, we play games to have fun. Is that why you play the game? Or is it to prove a point, to emphasize your opinion, to empower your own position, to validate your own worth, or to seek security for your future? If you participate for any of these reasons, you're in for a huge disappointment. Those kinds of results can't be generated by winning a game. Granted, they sometimes appear to be part of the benefit package of being first place, but don't let the glamor of the first place award deceive you. Ask anyone who has the big trophy if it brought them an anxiety-free utopia. Did it solve all of their problems? Did it magically open the door to all future success?

If anything, it probably adds to the responsibilities at hand. It carries with it the need to make it two in a row. It lends itself to the "I'll bet you can't do it again" syndrome. From the opening whistle to the final gun, play the game one-hundred percent. Once it is over, you can't continue to play the game any longer. You can't take the game home with you, carry it over to the next day or the next week—that kind of thinking is pointless. You can take home the value of the experience; you can evaluate your performance and use this data in preparation for the next game, and the next game, and the next game.

Nobody except your team-mates will pay any attention to you if you carry your victory trophy to another game; it's worthless, only a memento to remind you of the experience.

## WHAT'S THE PURPOSE OF COMPETITION?

You may be asking, "If all of this is true, why get involved?" The opportunity to grow is immeasurable when people of similar interests gather and openly share their knowledge and expertise. Performance is a learning process in itself. The excitement of everyday life is based on achieving pre-set goals. Don't you want to better yourself each day? Aren't you more satisfied when you discover some new information to add to your idea bank? Isn't it great when you meet a stranger and develop a friendship for the future? Is personal improvement a part of your life? If any or all of these happen as a result of your involvement in a competition, are you going to let a subjective score cancel any of the real value at hand?

The true champion walks away from every situation with more knowledge than he/she had at the onset of the event, because they see that everything else is just a game. People who choose not to play the game are simply playing the game of not playing—which, in turn, generates the same opinions and anxieties.

As music educators and students of music, we have a tremendous responsibility and a great opportunity to see that the key for making our game valuable to the players is through cooperation. Let's not lose perspective of our need for one another; of our great potential when we work together. Let us support our friends when the emotion of the moment distorts a clear view of what all of us are striving to bring to music education.

It's up to you. Only you can determine winning and losing in any game. There's not a judge anywhere who can take that responsibility off your shoulders. If you let them, you'll be sorely disappointed and confused about your next move forward. Opinions rate about eight on my own so-what-scale. (Now you can bet, someone has an opinion about my opinion scale.)

You're in charge of you; and that same you is in charge of your program. Do yourself and your program a favor and take charge. Strengthen your weaknesses, strengthen your strengths, and quit worrying about what the other guy says—it's just an opinion. Pinochle, anyone?

*"This story is about four people named Every-
body, Somebody, Anybody, and Nobody. There
was an important job to be done and Everybody was asked to do it. Everybody was sure
that Somebody would do it. Anybody could
have done it, but Nobody did it. Somebody got
angry about that, because it was Everybody's
job. Everybody thought that Anybody could do
it, and Nobody realized that Everybody
wouldn't do it. It ended up that Everybody
blamed Somebody when actually Nobody
should have been blamed by Anybody."*

# The True Value
# of Competition

If you are in the game of competition to win a trophy, then
you may find yourself sensing a great deal of frustration as you go
through the process of preparation-production-performance, particularly if, after all of that effort, you end up without a trophy.
Ouch! It's so easy to get caught up in that attitude of, "You mean
I did all of that work, and didn't even get a trophy?"

It's also a dead end street. Warning: If that sounds even vaguely
familiar, it may be time to readjust your thinking and reset your
priorities in terms of the true value of competition; otherwise, you
may be in store for a very depressing journey which has no final

destination except a more depressing journey.

Why do you compete? Is it to prove something to someone else? If so, you are destined to spend your whole life trying to satisfy another person. Shouldn't we be going through this effort to prove something to ourselves; to reach new levels of attainment and personal growth; to stretch our present talent level to new heights of accomplishment and self-satisfaction? Regardless of the outcome of any contest, if we do not feel we have gained through the experience, then why do we subject ourselves to a potentially damaging environment in the first place?

Far too often, people leave a competition expressing anger, disgust, frustration, revenge, blame, bitterness, hostility, and a host of other negative emotions. Is it worth it? Obviously not. As a result of this win-at-all-costs attitude, we often find the performers, instructors, even the audience participating from the vantage point of "We'll win by beating everyone else," which is a behavioral pattern of insecurity: "I'll make myself look better by making everyone else look worse." When we approach anything from that perspective, the negatives tend to feed themselves and the damaging emotions compound. After a length of time, this self-destructive behavior will result in the disappearance of the will to compete. In other words: "We quit!" Losing in its ultimate state: quitting, giving up, walking away, avoiding the game.

The word competition is derived from the French word *competere* which means to bring together. Let's suppose we approached every event with the understanding that we were bringing together different groups so that each person involved could learn from everyone else while putting forth his or her best effort to share with everyone else. The performers would agree to give their best effort to the performance. The instructors would agree to seek every opportunity to make their performers aware of new information which could improve them, and the audience would agree to be a great audience for every performance. Now, we have people participating out of desire to succeed instead of the fear of failure. With everyone supporting each other, the object of the competition becomes twofold: to give one's very best effort and to support everyone else to give his or her best effort. From this vantage point: I win when you win because I was, through my support of you, part of the reason for your success. Of course you will also win when I win. Everyone wins; nobody loses. Personal satisfaction runs high, and everyone is eager to participate and improve in the game. We all like to be participants in the games we can win. Along with this double win situation, we pick up the extra benefits of cooperation, dedication, sportsmanship, new friendships, and an eagerness to become more adept in both facets of the competition: performing and supporting.

Perhaps this seems just a bit too simple. It is if you put any stock in the meanings and ratings beyond a mere scorekeeping measure. The actual outcome of the competition cannot compare to the value of the learning experience for the participants unless we continue to pretend that it does mean something. The only possible meaning that it could have is in relationship to puffing up the ego a bit more, which, of course, is just another way of feeding insecurity. When this happens, we see young people, after giving their all, walk away from a competition dejected and hurt because they came in 2nd; behaving as though they had lost instead of celebrating the fact that they performed their best ever.

If judges were never wrong and performance conditions would remain absolutely stable for every group, and the human factor for every performer, instructor, and fan could be fine-tuned to always be predictably the same (which, of course, is impossible), we would still be comparing apples to grapefruits to blueberries. It is ludicrous to think anyone can do that and be certain. Look at the variables: size of group, style of music, color of uniforms, difference in visual structure, age of performers, economic support in the community, amount of rehearsal time, size of the practice facility, etc., etc., etc. Why even in sports, they have far more objective scoring methods: ball through the hoop, over the line, into the net, through the goalposts, out of the park. These can be measured.

How does one compare a flag routine for "Festive Overture" to a pom-pon routine for "Caravan"? One does the best one can, knowing the value lies in the suggestion input, not in the numerical score. Let us keep in mind our responsibility to:

Support rather than tear down.

To educate rather than criticize.

To appreciate rather than humiliate.

To encourage rather than discourage.

To have the courage to stand and cheer for everyone.

Real champions never have to tell anybody. We all sense it in their style of life, because they make us feel like winners too. Together we all can win. Sounds like a great way to play. Can we count you in? Then let the games begin!

# About the Author

Tim Lautzenheiser is a well-known name in the music education world as a: teacher, clinician, author, composer, consultant, adjudicator, and, above all, a trusted friend to anyone interested in helping young people develop a desire for excellence.

His own career involved ten years of successful college band directing at: Northern Michigan University, University of Missouri, and New Mexico State University. During this time, Tim developed nationally acclaimed groups in all area of the instrumental and vocal field. Although every organization from Symphonic Wind Ensemble to Swing Choir was seen as a trend-setter by many of his colleagues, he is best known for his programs dealing with positive attitude, student motivation, and effective leadership training.

After serving three years in the music industry, he created Attitude Concepts for Today, Inc. to meet the many requests for workshops, seminars, and convention speaking engagements.

Tim serves on several of today's educational advisory boards and is also an officer in several professional educational organizations. His work represents a positive blend of realism and idealism, and his tested formula for achieving personal happiness is being successfully proven by many people from coast to coast.